Awakening to the Tao

Awakening to the Tao

Liu I-ming

Translated from the Chinese
by Thomas Cleary

Shambhala

Boston & London

1988

Shambhala Publications, Inc.
Horticultural Hall
300 Massachusetts Avenue
Boston, Massachusetts 02115
www.shambhala.com

15 14 13 12 11 10 9
Printed in the United States of America

♾ This edition is printed on acid-free paper that meets the American National Standards Institute Z39.48 Standard.

Distributed in the United States by Random House, Inc., and in Canada by Random House of Canada Ltd

Library of Congress Cataloging-in-Publication Data

Liu, I-ming, 18th cent.
Awakening to the Tao.

1. Taoism. I. Cleary, Thomas E., 1949—

II. Title.
BL1920.L57 1988 181'.09514 88-17478
ISBN 0-87773-447-X (pbk.)

Contents

Preface

The Tao is the Way, the Way behind all ways, the principle underlying all principles, the fact underlying all facts. Taoism, in its broadest sense, is the search for truth and reality. In a narrower sense, it is the original knowledge tradition of China, but the narrowness of this definition is growing more acute day by day, as Taoism has already in the last couple of centuries extended some of its influence in the West to nearly as diverse an array of areas of human interest as it has in the East.

In English today we have books on Taoism and investment, Taoism and management, Taoism and health, Taoism and medicine, Taoism and sex, Taoism and science, Taoism and psychology, Taoism and art, Taoism and life, Taoism and war, Taoism and education, Taoism and society, Taoism and every sort of illuminism and religion.

This book, *Awakening to the Tao,* is none of these but includes something of all of them, and more—over a hundred methods of attaining reality as a fully conscious human being. According to the Zen masters of ancient times, when you awaken to that unique Way at the crossroads of all ways, you then hold the key to all ways, and can succeed in any of those ways you choose to practice.

Translator's Introduction

Awakening to the Tao is a collection of meditations formulated by Liu I-ming, one of the most adept Taoist writers of early modern times. Written in a simple, explicit style, it uses natural and mythical phenomena as metaphors illustrating the principles and practices of Taoism.

Born around 1737, Liu writes that he first became interested in Taoism during his early teens. According to his own account, he visited all sorts of supposed teachers and studied at random for several years. In his late teens he became gravely ill, and for the first time realized the uselessness of all he had studied.

Liu's illness did not respond to medical treatment, gradually worsening until he had become a complete invalid. At that point, he had the fortune to meet a "Real Human," a genuine Taoist adept, who was able to cure him. Now totally committed to seeking the Tao, Liu left home at the age of nineteen to travel in search of true learning.

About three years after embarking on this pilgrimage, Liu met someone he calls the Old Man of the Valley of the Crypts, whom he thereafter regarded as his teacher. This old man explained to him the fallacies in the aberrant practices of the ever popular pseudo-Taoist cults Liu had naturally encountered, and passed on the essential psychological teaching of true Taoism.

In later years, Liu was to mention this momentous event over and over in taking his stand against deviant practices and approaches to Taoism. There is nothing unique in this, of course, as similar warnings about sidetracks occur time and again in Taoist classics going back over two thousand years. If nothing else, this aspect of Taoist history testifies to the persistence of certain fascinations and the chronic lack of information among cultists.

After opening young Liu's mind to the central point of Taoism, the old man sent him home to finish his social duties and study the Taoist alchemical classics. Neglect of social life in youth and lack of sufficient grounding in the principles of mysticism were two of the major defects that great latter-day Taoists have repeatedly pointed out in aberrant pseudo-mystics.

Accordingly, Liu I-ming made a thorough investigation of the sacred literature of Taoism, Confucianism, and Buddhism. His later writings show a combined knowledge of alchemy and Zen Buddhism unequaled in his time, but his literary studies did not satisfy him at the time. His own explanation is that he left his teacher too soon. This resulted in twelve years of doubt and uncertainty.

During this unsettled period, Liu spent four years living in Beijing, the northern capital, two years in central China, three years in the far northwest, and four years wandering around. All this, in his own words, was on account of his search for truth. He studied spiritual writings every day, but still could not resolve his uncertainty.

Finally in 1772 Liu met his second teacher, whom he calls the Old Man of the Immortals' Station. Liu describes his experience under the old man's tutelage as like being raised from the bottom of an immeasurably deep pit to the top of an immeasurably high mountain. Freed from doubt forever, Liu now felt as though he "saw the whole world in the palm of his hand and encountered the Tao wherever he was."

After sudden enlightenment comes gradual application, and Liu further reports two profound and encompassing spiritual experiences that took place in 1776 and 1780. Then, "harmonizing enlightenment to assimilate with the world"—again in accord with classic principles—he spent many more years practicing concealment in company, traveling to various places and working at various jobs and professions while continuing his inner refinement.

Even after these experiences, Liu does not seem to have begun writing on Taoism until the 1790s, when he was already nearly sixty. He continued to write until around 1826, a period of nearly thirty years.

During this time he wrote matchless commentaries on Taoist classics such as *The Book of Changes*, *Understanding Reality*, *Triplex Unity*, *The Yin Convergence Classic*, *Four Hundred Words on the Gold Pill*, *Tapping the Lines*, *The Hundred Character Inscription*, *The Rootless Tree*, and *Journey to the West*.[1]

Liu also composed numerous essays, poems, and songs of his own, likewise employing the vocabulary of Taoist alchemy in psychological translation and expounding the essence of Taoism with unprecedented clarity. *Awakening to the Tao* is one of Liu's own compositions. Dating from 1816, when he was nearly eighty years old, it encapsulates a lifetime of work and contemplation in over a hundred brilliant opuscules.

NOTE

1. The well-known *Book of Changes (I Ching*, or *Yijing*, or *Zhouyi)* is one of the fundamental texts of Taoism, used to illustrate a complete cycle of development.

Understanding Reality (Wuzhen pian) and *Triplex Unity (Cantongqi)* are the two greatest alchemical texts and are called the ancestors of alchemical literature by the Complete Reality schools of Taoism.

The Yin Convergence Classic (Yinfujing) is even more ancient than *The Book of Changes*. It is attributed to the Yellow Emperor himself, one of the greatest figures of prehistoric Taoism, who is thought to have lived nearly five thousand years ago. Secular scholars believe it dates back at least to the Shang dynasty, roughly the second millennium B.C.E., on the grounds that there is already commentary on the classic from that period. This text has been interpreted in many ways; some regard it as a text on the art of warfare, while others regard it as a spiritual classic on a par with the Tao Te Ching.

Four Hundred Words on the Gold Pill (Jindan Sibaizi) is a seminal alchemical classic by the same author as *Understanding Reality*.

Tapping the Lines (Qiaoyao ge) and *The Hundred Character Inscription (Baizi bei)* are poems by the great Ancestor Lu, grandfather of the Complete Reality movement.

The Rootless Tree (Wugenshu) is a collection of poems by the fabled Zhang (Chang) Sanfeng, legendary originator of Absolute Boxing, alchemist capable of producing both material and spiritual gold, exposer of charlatans and dummies, and all-around Taoist wizard.

Journey to the West (Xiyouji) is one of the Four Extraordinary Books of the Ming dynasty, four great novels used as media extraordinaire for Taoist teaching in the secular society of post-Mongol times.

The following texts have been translated into English. *The Book of Changes*, with Liu's commentary, is in *The Taoist I Ching* (Boston and London: Shambhala, 1986). *Understanding Reality*, with Liu's commentary, is under its original title (Honolulu: University of Hawaii Press, 1988). *Four Hundred Words on the Gold Pill* is in *The Inner Teachings of Taoism* (Boston and London: Shambhala, 1987). The others are in a forthcoming anthology.

PART ONE

Contemplations

The Height of Heaven, the Thickness of Earth

The body of heaven is extremely high. Open, round, immeasurable, it is boundlessly vast. Covering everything, containing everything, it produces myriad beings without presuming on its virtue, it bestows blessings on myriad beings without expectation of reward. Whether people are respectful or insincere, supportive or antagonistic, is left up to them. Whether people are good or bad, attractive or repulsive, and whether creatures are violent and stubborn or docile and obedient, they are allowed to be so of themselves, without any contrivance.

The earth is very thick. Lowly, below all else, it bears everything and nurtures all beings. It can bear even the weight of the great mountains, and it can endure even the erosive force of great waters. It tolerates being pierced by plants and trees, and it submits to the tread of birds and beasts. It does not mind being cheapened by pollution.

What I realize as I observe this is the Tao of emulating heaven and earth. If people can be open-minded and magnanimous, be receptive to all, take pity on the old and the poor, assist those in peril and rescue those in trouble, give of themselves without seeking reward, never bear grudges, look upon others and self impartially, and realize all as one, then people can be companions of heaven.

If people can be flexible and yielding, humble, with self-control, entirely free of agitation, cleared of all volatility, not angered by criticism, ignoring insult, docilely accepting all hardships, illnesses, and natural disasters, utterly without anxiety or resentment when faced with danger or adversity, then people can be companions of earth.

With the nobility of heaven and the humility of earth,

one joins in with the attributes of heaven and earth and extends to eternity with them.

The Shining of the Sun and Moon

The way the sun works, it climbs into the sky in the daytime, thus illuminating the outward, then goes behind the earth at night, thus illuminating the inward. The way the moon works, in the first half of its cycle it produces light, thus illuminating the outward, then in the last half of its cycle it withdraws it light, thus nurturing the inward. Sun and moon, illuminating outside and inside, are all one light.

What I realize as I observe this is the Tao of using illumination. If people can use illumination outwardly, be careful about what they say and do, refrain from any inappropriate conduct, not dwell on anything but the Tao, not be distorted by the power of sensuality, intoxicants, and material goods, not be seduced by wealth or status, success or fame, not be stained by mundane feelings connected to worldly situations, then they can illuminate the outward as do the sun and moon.

If people can use illumination inwardly, do away with falsehood and maintain truthfulness, leave confusion and return to reality, learn to master emotions, clear up feelings, clean the mind, melt away the human mentality and activate the awareness of Tao, carefully avoiding even the slightest errant thought, then they can illumine the inward as do the sun and moon.

When the inward and the outward are illumined, and all is clear, you are one with the light of sun and moon. When developed to its ultimate state, this is a round luminosity which nothing can deceive, the subtle body of a unified spirit, pervading the whole universe. Then you have the same function as the sun and moon.

Thunder and Wind

Thunder is fierce, intense, and strong; wind is gradual, far-reaching, and soft. When wind and thunder combine, then there is soft gentleness in the midst of hard intensity, and there is hard intensity in the midst of soft gentleness. Hardness and softness complement each other.

What I realize as I observe this is the Tao of balanced harmonization of hardness and softness. When people practice the Tao to develop character, dealing with events and society, if they are always hard they will be impetuous and aggressive, excessively impatient, so their actions will lack perseverance and their keenness will be blunted. Then again, if people are always soft, they will vacillate, fearful and ineffective, and be too weak to succeed in their tasks. That softness is useless.

If people can be firm in decision and flexible in gradual practice, neither hurrying nor lagging, neither aggressive nor weak, with hardness and softness balancing each other, achieving balance and harmony, then they will benefit wherever they go. If they study the Tao in this way, eventually they will surely understand the Tao. If they practice the Tao in this way, eventually they will surely realize the Tao.

Therefore a classic written by a sage says, "Balance is the mainstay of the world, harmony is the way the world arrives on the Tao. Achieving balance and harmony, heaven and earth are in their places therein, myriad beings grow up therein." Such is the importance of the Tao of balance and harmony.

The Alternation of the Four Seasons

Spring, summer, autumn, winter—these are the four seasons. In spring things sprout, in summer things grow, in autumn things are harvested, in winter things are stored. Each has its turn, then passes on; when the cycle is completed, it begins again, so that the four seasons are linked together in a continuum.

What I realize as I observe this is the Tao of mutual causation, of subtraction and addition. Now what I mean by subtraction here is the subtraction of excess in strength and volatility, and what I mean by addition is addition to fill the lack caused by pliability and weakness. Being strong without letting strength go too far, being flexible without becoming ineffective, strength is joined to flexibility and flexibility is applied with strength.

Strength and flexibility matching each other, yin and yang matching each other, it is possible to be high or low, great or small; it is possible to advance or withdraw, to go along or oppose. Adapting uninhibitedly, indirectness and directness working parallel, one then merges with the order of the four seasons. Changing freely, there is a heaven and earth in one's own body, a Creation in one's own mind, yet one is not constrained by heaven, earth, and Creation.

The Moon Borrows the Sun's Light

The moon is originally pure yin, without yang—it only gives off light after borrowing the sun's rays. The waxing and waning of the moonlight depends on the position and proportion of the sunlight.

What I realize as I observe this is the Tao of borrowing yang to transmute yin. The human body is originally pure yin without yang—it must borrow the yang of other to become yang.

"Other" means everything other than oneself—sky and earth, sun and moon, myriad beings, myriad things. The so-called "yang of other" is the primordial open unified energy, which is the undying human being.

This energy is innate, but as it mixes with acquired conditioning it gradually gets scattered among the sky and earth, sun and moon, myriad beings and things, and is not one's own anymore, belonging to other.

If you know this energy is in other, and gradually steal it back to return it to self, restoring the existence of the nonexistent, regaining what had been lost, that is like the moon shining by borrowing the light of the sun. This is the celestial mechanism of taking over Creation and reversing yin and yang.

Steadying the Furnace and Setting Up the Cauldron

When alchemists cook medicines, first they must steady the furnace and set up the cauldron. The quality of the cauldron is firmness, whereby the medicine is contained; the quality of the furnace is flexibility, whereby the firing is operated. If the cauldron is not strong, the medicine is easily lost; if the furnace is not steady, the fire flies off at random.

What I realize as I observe this is the Tao of refining body and mind. Firmness of determination in cultivating the Tao is the cauldron. Becoming stronger with perseverance, never turning back even though foiled a hundred times, being imperturbable, unwavering—this is "setting up the cauldron." Alert observation at all times is the furnace. Working gradually, serenely, unpressured—this is "steadying the furnace."

When the cauldron and furnace are stabilized properly, you burn away the acquired habits that have become compulsive over the course of personal history, thus bringing to light the original state of completeness, sloughing off all acquired pollutants.

When the slag is gone and the gold is pure, you get rid of the old and take the new. Now you change the furnace and cauldron, and set aside the tongs and bellows, to do advanced work, melting the real gold down into liquid and frost, returning to the state before birth.

So it is that the alchemical classics and writings of the adepts consider steadying the furnace and setting up the cauldron the first priority.

Fire and Water Mirrors

A fire-making mirror is able to take fire from the sun, even at an immense distance. A water-collecting mirror is able to take water from the moon, even at a vast remove. This is because the energies of the fire and water mirrors are the same kind as those of the sun and moon.

What I realize as I observe this is the Tao of absorbing yin and yang. The yin and yang in the human being are originally combined into one energy; it is because of mixture with temporal conditioning that yin and yang separate. Once yin and yang have separated, the energy of life decreases day by day and the energy of death increases day by day. As the energy of life decreases more and more while the energy of death increases more and more, in the end there is only death.

If you know how to turn the light of awareness around to look within, using the artificial to cultivate the real, then in a moment yin and yang will merge and combine, spontaneously and effortlessly. If you realize this, it is near at hand; if not, it is far away. It is simply a matter of being willing to do it.

Dung Beetles

Dung beetles roll balls of dung, from which their offspring are born after a time. Balls of dung are originally dead things, with nothing in them, but by the communion of female and male energies joining into one energy that does not disperse, the spirit congeals and the energy coagulates, and is thus able to produce substance and form where there was no substance or form.

What I realize as I observe this is the Tao of producing being from within nonbeing. People are born with the two energies of heaven and earth, yin and yang, so they have these two energies, yin and yang, within their bodies. If people can bring the yang to the yin, and cause the yin to follow the yang, yin and yang adhere to each other. In the midst of ecstatic trance there is a point of living potential, coming into being from nonbeing, whereby the spiritual embryo can be formed and the spiritual body can be produced.

When this practice reaches its consummation, you break through space and have a body outside your body. Walking on the sun and moon without form, penetrating metal and stone without hindrance, you transcend Creation.

Lead and Quicksilver

In material alchemy, when quicksilver is exposed to fire, it flies off. When lead is put into quicksilver, the quicksilver is stabilized; and they combine to form a mass without volatility.

What I realize as I observe this is the Tao of controlling yin by means of yang. The human mind is mercurial and unpredictable; it gives rise to emotions about what it experiences, and stirs up confusion after exposure to external influences. This is like quicksilver flying off when exposed to fire.

If the mind of Tao is always present, warding off danger, and one is always aware, then the human mind has no room to arise. This is like quicksilver being stabilized by lead.

If you then go on to work diligently at increasing the positive energy of the mind of Tao while reducing the negative energy of the human mind, increasing and reducing until no more increase or reduction is possible, then the human mind dies and the mind of Tao is stable.

The seed of realization is then in your hands, and with it you can become a sage, an immortal, a buddha. At this point the foundation of essence and life is established. Now if you go on to do advanced work, you will surely attain profound self-realization.

Planting Wheat and Planting Flax

If you plant wheat, you get wheat; if you plant flax, you get flax. Flax does not produce wheat, wheat does not produce flax—the seeds are different.

What I realize as I observe this is the Tao of cause and effect in action. If people's thought is good, their actions and deeds are good, so they will surely receive blessings. If people's thought is bad, their actions and deeds are also bad, so they will surely bring on misfortune.

Good and bad thought are the cause of events, receiving blessings and bringing on misfortune are the effect of events. When there is a cause, it will surely have an effect. It cannot be that the fruit of good seed is not good, nor can it be that the fruit of bad seed is not bad. The consequences of good and bad are like shadows following forms, certain and invariable.

It is all a matter of choosing between planting good and planting evil, distinguishing what is good and what is bad.

Therefore superior people consider the beginning when they do things; being careful about things in the beginning, they are able to complete them in the end.

Grafting Peaches and Grafting Plums

When a peach tree is old, graft on a young branch and it will again bear peaches. When a plum tree is old, graft on a young branch and it will again bear plums. This is because even when a tree is old it still has energy in its roots.

What I realize as I observe this is the Tao of grafting when people grow old. People age because they indulge in emotions and passions—a hundred worries affect their minds, myriad affairs weary their bodies. Expending their vitality, exhausting their spirit, they take the false to be real and take misery for happiness.

Their living potential is cut away to the point where it nearly perishes entirely, their nature is disturbed and their life is shaken. Because the root is unstable, they grow old and die. This cannot be attributed to fate, for they bring it on themselves.

If people know enough to regret their errors and change, cut off emotional entanglements, get rid of addictions to intoxicants, sensuality, and possessions, look upon wealth and status as like ephemeral clouds, regard power and profit as like bandits and enemies, then everything will be empty for them, and they will not be attached to anything.

Concentrating the energy like a baby, being abstemious, storing the vitality and nurturing the spirit, getting rid of illusion and returning to reality, fostering the growth of the root at all times, walking every step on the right path, increasing true thought and diminishing false thought, truly sincere within and without, integrated with the design of nature, they can thereby be rejuvenated.

This is like the way of grafting a young branch onto an old tree. An ancient adept said, "Even at the age of seventy or eighty, as long as you still have one breath left in you, restoration is possible." This is true.

A Hair Turning into a Water Snake

If a hair falls into a puddle of water and is exposed to hot sunshine, it takes on the form of a water snake. Why is this? Though a hair is a dead thing, when it is moistened by water and warmed by the sun, the moisture and heat coalesce into an energy with a subtle potential that produces movement. Therefore the hair swims around in the water like a snake.

What I realize as I observe this is the Tao of stabilizing the root and solidifying life. The yang energy in people is associated with fire, while the yin energy is associated with water. When yin and yang combine, the energies of water and fire balance each other. There is a point of living potential there, which is at first vague but becomes clearly apparent, producing life without cease.

The declining can thereby flourish, the weak can thereby become strong, the lifeless can solidify life, the short-lived can extend their life span. This is the way to deepen the root and make the stem firm, to live on the plane of eternity.

The Crane and the Tortoise

The crane is good at nurturing the spirit, so it lives for a thousand years. The tortoise is good at nurturing energy, so it can survive a century without food.

What I realize as I observe this is the Tao of prolonging life. If people are able to humbly lower themselves, to be yielding, plain, and sincere, not wasting energy but always nurturing energy, then they will be full of energy. If people can be free from cogitation and rumination, have few desires and little ambition, not belabor their spirit but always maintain their spirit, then their spirit will be complete.

When energy is full and the spirit is complete, the root is stable and the foundation is secure. Thus you can extend your life span, prolonging life without deterioration. The crane and the tortoise can live long, even though one only keeps its spirit complete and one only keeps its energy complete; how much the more so when both spirit and energy are kept complete—how could you fail to live long?

The Freezing of Water and the Melting of Ice

Water freezes into ice when it is cold, ice melts into water when it is warm. What I realize as I observe this is the Tao of becoming either a sage or an ordinary person.

At first, human nature is basically good. There is originally no distinction between the sage and the ordinary person. It is because of the energy of accumulated habits that there comes to be a difference between sages and ordinary people.

If one practices what is good, one does not lose the divinely bestowed nature, and thus becomes a sage. If one practices what is not good, one loses the divinely bestowed nature, and thus becomes an ordinary person.

If those who are not good know enough to change their ways and turn from error to goodness, get rid of perversity and return to rectitude, and imbue themselves with goodness, then they can restore the divinely bestowed nature, and even though they have been ordinary people they can become sages.

If those who are originally good do not know enough to be careful and prudent, and instead become affected by external influences and become habituated to what is not good, then they lose the divinely bestowed nature, and even though they have been sages they become ordinary people.

Those who are good are like water, those who are not good are like ice. The fact that sages can become ordinary people and ordinary people can become sages is like the fact that water can become ice and ice can become water. Therefore the path of great learning lies in the clarification of the quality of illumination, and in resting in the ultimate good.

The Flourishing of Trees, the Extension of Streams

When roots of a tree are deep, its leaves naturally flourish. When the source of a stream is abundant, its flow naturally extends far. This is the way it is with that which has a basis.

What I realize as I observe this is the Tao of preserving and maintaining the fundamental. The original vitality, original energy, and original spirit of human beings are the wellspring of essence and life. When the original vitality is undiminished, the body is complete. When the original energy is undamaged, life is secure. When the original spirit is unobscured, the essence is clear.

When the body is whole, life is secure, and the essence is clear, then myriad things cannot move you, Creation cannot constrain you; your nature and destiny are up to you, not up to Heaven.

This is like leaves flourishing when the roots of the tree are deep, the flow of a stream extending far when its source is abundant. When the basis is established, the Way develops; the living potential is ever present and never ceases.

Most people, however, do not know enough to preserve and maintain the fundamental; instead they act on the outgrowths, imagining falsely that they will thereby attain the Tao. This is like looking for fish in a tree—it will turn out to be in vain after all. Is this not foolish?

The Heart of the Pine, the Joints of Bamboo

The heart of the pine is solid, the joints of bamboo are hard; therefore they do not wither in the cold of winter, but continue to flourish even through snow and frost.

What I realize as I observe this is the Tao of establishing life through cultivation and discipline. If people can avoid what is shameful, be serious, sincere, and impartial, then their hearts will be solid. When the heart is solid, one cannot be corrupted by wealth or status, one cannot be moved by poverty or lowliness, one cannot be suppressed by authority or force.

Dealing with events fearlessly, undisturbed by difficulty, the fortunes or misfortunes one may encounter are up to others, while the creation of life is up to oneself.

If people can cultivate themselves and control their affairs, resting in the proper place, standing firm and unmoving, then they will be regulated and strong. Being regulated and strong, they do not act in any way that is improper, they do not dwell on anything but the Tao, they do not do anything unjust.

Accepting the bitter along with the sweet, able to lead and able to follow, accepting both life and death, always responsive yet always tranquil, not moved by things, firm of heart and strong in discipline, one can thereby handle ease, one can thereby handle danger, one can thereby act, one can thereby rest, one can thereby change adaptively without hindrance, unfixed to any given pattern, uninhibited in any way.

Wood and Charcoal, Clay and Brick

When wood is exposed for a long time it rots, but if it is fired into charcoal it will never rot. Water and earth combine to make clay, which dissolves in the rain; fire it into brick, however, and it will last indefinitely.

What I realize as I observe this is the Tao of firing to cultivate reality. The reason people are unable to attain the Tao is because they have not yet been "fired" in the furnace of Creation.

If one walks with every step on the ground of reality in the furnace of Creation, experiencing everything that comes along, being in the doorway of life and death without wavering, like gold that becomes brighter the more it is fired, like a mirror that becomes clearer the more it is polished, fired and polished to a state of round brightness, clean nakedness, bare freedom, where there is neither being nor nonbeing, where others and self all become empty, then one will be mentally and physically sublimated, and will merge with the Tao in reality. This is like wood and clay passing through fire to become charcoal and brick, never to decay.

The Flesh and Hair of Corpses

When a corpse has been buried for a long time, any flesh that has not thoroughly decomposed becomes a pernicious influence that is harmful to people. When the hair of a corpse has been exposed to moisture and heat for a long time, it becomes foxfire, which deceives people.

What I realize as I observe this is the Tao of liberation from a great affliction. In the human body, upper and lower, inside and out, there is nothing that is not a pernicious influence and deceptive force.

Outwardly, the eyes, ears, nose, mouth, tongue, and body gang up and beckon external ills. Inwardly, the heart, liver, spleen, lungs, and kindeys link up to produce errant thoughts. These inner and outer depradations cut away natural reality, until ultimately they destroy life. The extent of the injury and deception they work on people is impossible to express in words.

Laozi (Lao-tzu) said, "The reason I have a great affliction is that I have a body. Had I no body, where would affliction come from?" So we know that this body is our great affliction. If we can escape this affliction, then that which is unafflicted will remain. Only that which is unafflicted is the true self.

Getting rid of affliction requires first that we recognize the true self. Only when we recognize the true self do we realize that the body is other. The other and self are unconnected to one another. Getting rid of the other by means of the self is quite simple, and requires no expenditure of effort.

Nevertheless, many practitioners of Taoism take the other for the self, take affliction to be reality. Emotionally attached to it, they take this ghost for a neighbor and refuse to give it up. There are even ignoramuses who do inner exercises based on this great affliction, imagining they will attain the Tao thereby. People like this are all taking the servant for the master, taking a thief to be one's child. Not only are they unable to get rid of the affliction, they even increase the affliction. No wonder they are frantic all their lives, only to end up falling into destruction.

Water Rising, Fire Descending

Water is basically cool, fire is basically hot. When fire rises and water descends, water and fire are in different places and cannot offset each other. If water rises and fire descends, then that which is hot does not flame, and that which is cold can become warm.

What I realize as I observe this is the Tao of separation and joining of yin and yang. The yang energy in people is firm; firmness without restraint turns into aggressiveness, like fire rising. Yin energy is flexible; flexibility without support becomes too weak, like water descending. When firmness and flexibility do not balance each other, solitary yin cannot give life, isolated yang cannot foster growth—so the living energy ceases.

If one is firm without being aggressive, using firmness with flexibility, that is like fire being below. If one is flexible without being weak, supporting flexibility with firmness, that is like water being above. When firmness and flexibility are balanced, yin and yang are in harmony; essence and sense merge, water and fire offset each other. This is what is called the inversion of water and fire.

Melon Seeds

Inside every melon are seeds, inside every seed is a germ. The germ is twofold, and within those two parts there is also a single heart. This heart is the point of living potential. The growth of a melon all comes from this. This is what is called the heart of heaven and earth.

What I realize as I observe this is the Tao of the living potential of yin and yang. Only when yin and yang join is there the germ of humanity; when there is the germ of humanity, it encompasses the heart of heaven and earth. If yin and yang do not combine, there is no germ of humanity; without the germ of humanity, there is no heart of heaven and earth.

The heart of heaven and earth is the basis of ongoing growth; those who attain this heart become sages, buddhas, immortals; those who lose this heart become animals, ghosts, demons. Whether one has this heart or lacks this heart is all a matter of whether yin and yang are separated or united.

If learners can blend yin and yang without partiality or bias, ending up in correct balance, then the heart of heaven and earth will reappear. When the heart of heaven appears, whatever is at hand is the Tao, wherever one walks is reality—the mainspring of Creation is in one's own grip.

Murky Water, Dusty Mirror

Murky water is turbid; let it settle and it clears. A dusty mirror is dim; clean it and it is bright.

What I realize as I observe this is the Tao of clarifying the mind and perceiving its essence.

The reason why people's minds are not clear and their natures are not stable is that they are full of craving and emotion. Add to this eons of mental habit, acquired influences deluding the mind, their outgrowths clogging up the opening of awareness—this is like water being murky, like a mirror being dusty. The original true mind and true essence are totally lost. The feelings and senses are unruly, subject to all kinds of influences, taking in all sorts of things, defiling the mind.

If one can suddenly realize this and change directions, wash away pollution and contamination, gradually remove a lifetime of biased mental habits, wandering thoughts and perverse actions, increasing in strength with persistence, refining away the dross until there is nothing more to be refined away, when the slag is gone the gold is pure. The original mind and fundamental essence will spontaneously appear in full, the light of wisdom will suddenly arise, and one will clearly see the universe as though it were in the palm of the hand, with no obstruction.

This is like murky water returning to clarity when settled, like a dusty mirror being restored to brightness when polished. That which is fundamental is as ever without any lack.

The Heat of Movement, the Coldness of Stillness

Generally speaking, when people are active, this gives rise to heat; when people sit quietly, this gives rise to cold. When one is cold, if one moves about this will again produce heat. When one is hot, if one sits still this will again produce coldness. In other words, cold and heat do not depend on the weather but on the person.

What I realize as I observe this is the Tao of taking over the creativity of yin and yang. That which is strong is associated with yang, that which is yielding is associated with yin. If one is strong but not aggressive, humbly lowering oneself, then one will not be irritable but will be peaceful, and equanimous. If one is yielding but not weak, deliberate in action, then one will not be ineffective but will ascend to high illumination.

Able to be strong, able to yield, according with truth and according with the time, knowing when to advance and when to withdraw, able to be great and able to be small, able to stop and able to step down, able to be passive and able to be active, one can thereby take over Creation, turn around life and death, reverse the mechanism of energy, leave death and go to life. This is like activity producing heat and quiet sitting producing cold; human power can reverse nature.

Earth Mounds, Giant Trees

A high earth mound is built up from the ground; a giant tree of enormous girth grows from a seed. This does not come about in a day and a night, but takes place gradually. What I realize as I observe this is the Tao of profound attainment of self-realization.

The matter of essence and life is the most important thing in the world. Keeping essence and life whole is the most difficult thing in the world. It cannot be done easily, and cannot be attained in one leap. It requires application to reality with every step, through everything one experiences.

Climbing from lowliness to the heights, penetrating from the shallows to the depths, gradually applying effort in an orderly manner, not counting the months and years, not losing heart, eventually one will reach fulfillment.

It is most important not to waste time vacillating, and not to give up halfway, as this will only leave you with unhappiness. This is especially true in that something that lasts forever without change can only be accomplished by long persistent effort.

If you start out diligently but end up slacking off, or indulge in idle imagination and hope thereby to keep essence and life whole and accomplish that which is rare in the world, you have no chance whatsoever of success. Therefore a sage said that people without constancy cannot even become seers or physicians, much less attain completeness of essence and life.

Filling Concavities, Wearing Away Protuberances

A concavity becomes full over a long period of time, while a protuberance wears away over a long period of time. This is because that which is empty is bound to be filled, and that which is high is bound to be lowered. What I realize as I observe this is the Tao of decrease and increase, of emptiness and fulfillment.

When people elevate and aggrandize themselves, confident of their talent and ability, strutting around as though they were sages, then others often detest them; time and again they bring error on themselves by self-satisfaction, and eventually they will fall below others, becoming anything but elevated. This is like a protuberance of earth gradually being worn away by people treading on it.

When people humble and minimize themselves, dismissing intellectuality, being modest and restrained, then others often respect them; time and again they benefit by emptying their hearts, and eventually will advance beyond others, becoming anything but low. This is like a concavity in the ground gradually filling by an accumulation of earth.

Therefore in the case of developed people, the loftier their path becomes the more humble their hearts are. Their virtue grows day by day, yet they become daily more circumspect, until all pride is gone and all agitation is dissolved.

Carp and Foxes

It is said that carp can turn into dragons and foxes can turn into fairies. This is because when the spirit is whole the form can change. What I realize as I observe this is the Tao of transformation by spiritual power.

Fish and foxes have partial energies of heaven and earth. What they depend on is only a part of consciousness. It is humans who are the most conscious of beings; they have the true energy of heaven and earth. In them the five forces are complete, the five virtues are inherent. They abide in the middle of the triad of heaven, earth, and humanity, and have the total capacity of heaven and earth.

If one can nurture the true energy of heaven and earth and preserve the harmonious energies of the five forces without partiality or imbalance, they merge into a single flow of energy. Then one has the creativity of heaven and earth, and can transform into a sage, change into an immortal. Physically and spiritually sublimated, one then merges into reality with the Tao, and is able to transform in countless ways, not only in appearance.

Transformations of a Spiritual Dragon

A dragon, as spiritual luminosity, can be large or small, can rise or descend, can disappear or appear, can penetrate rocks and mountains, can leap in the clouds and travel with the rain. How can it do all this? It is done by the activity of the spirit.

What I realize as I observe this is the Tao of inconceivable spiritual transmutation. The reason humans can be humans is because of the spirit. As long as the spirit is there, they live. When the spirit leaves, they die.

The spirit penetrates heaven and earth, knows the past and present, enters into every subtlety, exists in every place. It enters water without drowning, enters fire without burning, penetrates metal and rock without hindrance. It is so large that it fills the universe, so small that it fits into a hairtip. It is imperceptible, ungraspable, inexplicable, indescribable.

One who can use the spirit skillfully changes in accordance with the time, and therefore can share the qualities of heaven and earth, share the light of sun and moon, share the order of the four seasons, command nature in the primordial state, and serve nature in the temporal state. This is like the transformations of a spiritual dragon, which cannot be seen in the traces of form.

Dead Trees, Cold Ashes

When a tree is dead there is no flame when you burn it; when ashes are cold there is no warmth when you stir them. What I realize as I observe this is the Tao of transformation of temperament.

When people become temperamental, the harm is very great; the slightest offense sets them off into a rage. It damages nature and injures reason, so that they are unaware of their own greed and passion, they do not understand their own narrowness, they do not care about essential life, they are not mindful of life and death. The troubles this causes are not simple.

If one can master oneself and exercise restraint, turn back from inflexibility and become yielding, sweep away all anger, resentment, and annoyance, get rid of all contentiousness, change the aggressive and violent nature back into a gentle taciturn nature, concentrate the energy and make it flexible, empty the mind and nurture the spirit, be selfless and impersonal, not discriminate between self and others, view one's own body as having no such body, view one's mind as having no such mind, have no discrimination and no knowledge, and be empty and open, this is like dead wood not flaming when burnt, like cold ashes yielding no warmth when stirred.

One can thereby be in the midst of Creation without being influenced by Creation, be in the midst of yin and yang without being constrained by yin and yang.

Contact with Rouge, Contact with Soot

Something in prolonged contact with rouge eventually becomes red; something in prolonged contact with soot eventually becomes black. What I realize as I observe this is the Tao of habituation to good and bad.

When you live with good people, what you always hear are good words and what you always see are good actions. Hearing and seeing good words and actions over a long period of time plants good seeds in your mind, so that you spontaneously become accustomed to goodness.

When you live with bad people, what you always hear are bad words and what you always see are bad actions. Hearing and seeing bad words and bad actions over a long period of time plants bad seeds in your mind, so that you naturally become accustomed to badness.

Good and bad people are said to be so by nature, but most become so through habit. Therefore wise people choose their associates carefully.

The Natural Reality of the Infant

When an infant is first born, it has no conscious knowledge, no attachment to pleasures and possessions, no sentimental bonds. It knows nothing of wealth or poverty, has no ideas of self, person, being, or life. For the infant, everything is open—nothing defiles it, for it is indifferent, equanimous, purely natural.

What I realize as I observe this is the Tao of restoration of innocence. If people are able to radically wake up and turn around, shedding attachments to things, to dwell in the realm of nothingness and formlessness, to uproot the senses and objects conditioned by history and sweep away the force of habit acquired in the present life, letting go everywhere to be open and clear, pure and clean, then even if the body is old the nature is restored; outwardly one may be weak, but inwardly one is robust.

This is the restoration of youth, the original state of the infant. Otherwise, once natural reality is lost, even if one is physically strong and fat as a pig or an ox, what is the benefit?

Bellows

A bellows has holes on either side, and at the opening of each hole is a flap. Inside is empty, while the frame is straight. The emptiness inside is the essence, the straightness of the frame is the function. The two holes are the passages of exit and entry; the two flaps are the mechanism of opening and closing. As the frame is worked back and forth, taking in and pushing out, it empties without exhaustion, moves to produce wind, opening and closing naturally.

What I realize as I observe this is the Tao of the essence and function of cultivating reality. If people can be essentially empty within and be functionally straightforward in mind, without bias, without greed, letting the celestial design flow through them, then firmness and flexibility will match each other, action and stillness will combine appropriately, indirectness and directness will attain balance, and they can be passive or active in accordance with the situation.

Then people can share the same mechanism of energy as the sky, share the creativity of heaven and earth. This is like a bellows, inwardly empty with a straight frame, coming and going, breathing in and out naturally. As the working of energy does not cease, people can live long.

The Handle of the Big Dipper

It is said that where the handle of the Big Dipper points is auspicious, while where it sits is inauspicious. What I realize as I observe this is the Tao of turning around the working of energy.

The energy of strength in people may be likened to the handle of the Big Dipper in the sky: When the energy of strength is used outwardly, it is outwardly auspicious but inwardly inauspicious; when the energy of strength is used inwardly, it is inwardly auspicious but outwardly inauspicious. This is like the astrological belief that where the handle of the Big Dipper points is auspicious, while where it sits is inauspicious.

After people are born and get mixed up in temporal conditioning, their strength is all used outwardly in the struggle to prevail and the desire for power. They accept the false and abandon the real, which is injurious to the inner three treasures of vitality, energy, and spirit. Thus, beneficial energy is dispersed outwardly, while harmful energy is taken in. Over a long period of time the positive is exhausted and the negative becomes total—thus death is inevitable.

Therefore advanced people turn the dipper handle around, in the sense that they use strength inwardly to destroy debilitating influences, get rid of drainage through the senses, cut off entanglements and sweep away objects. Not letting the false damage the real, not letting externals disturb them inwardly, beneficial energy grows day by day, while harmful energy disappears day by day. Eventually beneficial energy is pure and harmful energy is gone, so that they are able to live long.

Lunatics and Drunkards

If a lunatic jumps over a fence, he may stumble, but he will not get hurt. If a drunkard falls from a cart, he may get hurt, but he will not die. Why is this? Because they are oblivious of their bodies.

What I realize as I observe this is the Tao of nurturing life and making the body whole. The life of human beings is dependent on the three treasures of vitality, energy, and spirit; when the three treasures are together, people live, and when the three treasures are scattered, people die. If you want to get the three treasures together, first you must be selfless. When selfless, the mind is open; when the mind is open, the three treasures do not leak away or dissipate. There is only increase, there cannot be decrease.

Increasing without decrease, increasing and increasing, one will become inwardly fulfilled. When inwardly fulfilled, the creative mechanism will live on unceasing. Lunatics and drunkards can even avoid death simply by forgetting their bodies; how much the more so is it possible to preserve life by completeness of spirit, fullness of energy, and stability of vitality.

Lifting the Rope, Lifting the Collar

When you straighten out a net, you lift the main rope; when you fold a robe, you pick it up by the collar. This is a way of saying that you start something at the point essential to the whole.

What I realize as I observe this is the Tao of preparing the basis of realization.

The mind is the master of the body, and is the basis upon which sagacity, enlightenment, and wizardry can be achieved. When the mind is quiet, all objects are silent; when the mind stirs, a jumble of thoughts arises at random.

If you can be empty and clear, with nothing whatsoever on your mind, not producing thoughts from within, not taking in things from without, always responsive yet always calm, always calm yet always responsive, then even if you are daily in the midst of excitement and agitation, your mind will be clear as a mirror and still as a lake, without dust, without waves. Then you will naturally be unaffected by circumstances.

Washing Out Gold, Sorting Out Jade

Washing gold out from sand and sorting jades out from rocks cannot be done by acting at random—these processes require intense effort and thoroughgoing work.

What I realize as I observe this is the Tao of practicing gradual cultivation.

The true treasure of the primordial is like gold, like jade; the artificial things that are temporally acquired are like sand and stone. When acquired artificialities bury the primordial treasure of reality, that is like sand and stone burying gold and jade.

Therefore, if you want to seek the primordial reality, you must shake off acquired artificiality. That which is real is the conscious root of the unified primordial energy; that which is artificial is the influence of all kinds of actions over time. This influence, plus the energies of the forces of the acquired personality and constitution, with accumulated leanings, buries the one reality within myriad artificialities.

Thus, since reality cannot be easily attained, it is necessary to use the power of gradual cultivation to shed the artificial in order that the real may appear. Shedding and shedding until there is nothing more to shed, you see, when everything artificial is gone, that the real is spontaneously clear right there before your eyes. This is like seeing the gold or the jade when the sand or pebbles are cleared away. This is the accomplishment of "sweetness after bitterness."

Drawing Water with a Well Sweep

When a well sweep draws water, the bucket goes down empty and comes up full, drawing water in a continuous cycle to water the fields.

What I realize as I observe this is the Tao of the twin functions of emptying and filling.

If people can empty their hearts and be humble towards others, they will receive benefits that will fill them within and elevate them beyond others. The more they become empty and humble, the more they are fulfilled and elevated.

Continually becoming empty, continually being fulfilled, continually becoming humble, continually being elevated, so that one is empty yet full, full yet empty, low yet high, high yet low, one attains to a state in which above and below are in communion, emptiness and fulfillment correspond.

Filled with the qualities of the Tao, those who reach this state never fail to ascend to lofty and clear perception. When it says in the *Book of Changes* "Accord is in lowliness—it is good to attend to people's psychological needs in detail," it is a general reference to the fact that the more elevated the path the humbler the mind.

The Flowers and Fruits of Plants and Trees

Plants and trees first flower and then produce fruit, each in its season. This is why they can live a long time. If they miss their season, this is a foresign of death, because it is abnormal.

What I realize as I observe this is the Tao of going along with time.

What human life depends on is spirit and energy. When events take place people cannot but respond to them, and when things come up they cannot but deal with them. Using events to control events, organizing things according to what is there, not looking forward to what has not come, not dwelling on what has passed, the spirit is not injured and the energy is not dissipated. This is like plants and trees flowering and fruiting in season; this is the enlivening path.

If people are greedy and passionate, ambitious and always conniving, forming strategies for events that are yet to come, clinging to events that have already passed, the spirit and energy become worn out. This is like plants and trees flowering and blooming out of season; this is the road to death.

Therefore wise people are as careful of their vitality and spirit as one would be of jewels. When they are used, they shine without dazzle; when put in storage, they are silent and still. Wise people act when it is appropriate to do so, stop when it is appropriate to stop. Action and stillness in their proper place, they do not damage the real with the artificial.

Effigies

Effigies made of wood or clay are basically inert, but if people sincerely worship them for a long time, miraculous effects ensue. What I realize as I reflect on this is the Tao of rising from death and returning to life.

People from all over the world take what is artificial to be real, and think what is misery is pleasurable. By day they roam among the objects of the world, by night they enter the realm of dream illusions. This is the road of death; there is no real life in it. The body may be alive, but the mind is already dead; one may exist physically yet be spiritually deceased. When this goes on day after day, year in and year out, positive energy is used up and only negative energy remains—how can death be avoided?

If you know the things of the world are all artificial, and experience an intense awakening, reverse your direction, and then are sincere and undivided, not thinking about anything but essence and life, being attentive and careful, guarding against insidious tendencies, over a long time your accomplishment will deepen; the mind will become spontaneously clear, the spirit will become spontaneously effective, inner thoughts will not arise, outer objects will not enter in, and there will be reality with no falsehood.

Then you can move sky and earth, conquer demons and spirits, take over Creation, overcome myriad things, level hell, ascend to heaven, open the door of life and shut the door of death, extend your years and enhance your life. Of this you can be sure.

Lamplight

When lamplight shines inside a room, then the room is light while outside is dark. When the lamp is moved outside, then outside is light while inside the room is dark.

What I realize as I observe this is the Tao of proper use of illumination.

People's intellect and knowlege are like the light of a lamp. If that light is mistakenly used outside, in a contentious and aggressive manner, aiming for name and gain, scheming and conniving day and night, thinking a thousand thoughts, imagining ten thousand imaginings, chasing artificial objects and losing the original source, light on the outside but dark inside, this will go on until the body is injured and life is lost.

If people give up artificiality and return to the real, dismiss intellectuality and cleverness, consider essential life the one matter of importance, practice inner awareness, refine the self and master the mind, observe all things with detachment so all that exists is empty of absoluteness, are not moved by external things and are not influenced by sensory experiences, being light inside and dark outside, they can thereby aspire to wisdom and become enlightened.

Light that does not dazzle progresses to lofty illumination; therefore a classic says, "The great sage appears ignorant, the great adept seems inept."

Wine from Mash, Gruel from Rice

To make wine you must use fermented mash; without fermentation mash does not make wine. To make gruel you must use rice; without rice you cannot make gruel. It is because fermented mash has the energy of wine to begin with that it can produce wine, and it is because rice is the essential part of the grain that it can make gruel—each accords with its own kind.

What I realize as I observe this is the Tao of the same kind of essence and life following each other.

Essence here means the natural essence, not temperament. It is the essence in which temperament is sublimated and dissolved. Life means the natural life, not a short or long span. It is the life which is not different, whether the span is short or long.

Those cultivating reality who want to cultivate essence and life must seek the seed of essence and life; and when they find the seed, they must cultivate it—only then can essence and life be perfected. When the wrong seed is cultivated, essence and life are instead damaged.

The seed is outside, yet is not a material substance. The seed is inside, yet is not bodily fluid or air. Anything that has form is not of a kind with our essence and life, and so cannot be used to realize essence and life.

If you want to know the true seed of essence and life, it is nothing but the original, innate, primal, true, unified energy. This energy is imperceptible and ungraspable; it cannot be found in the body, nor can it be found outside the body. It is not apart from the body, yet it is not attached to the body either. It is between ecstasy and trance, hidden in the realm of empty silence. Internalized, it is true emptiness; externalized, it is ineffable existence. It cannot be communicated in words, cannot be depicted in writing. If we were to insist on an illustration, it would simply be a circle. When names are forced on it, Confucians call it the absolute, Buddhists call it complete awareness, Taoists call it the gold pill.

The absolute, complete awareness, the gold pill—though there are three names, the actuality is one. This alone is the true seed of essence and life. To investigate principle means to investigate this true seed. To fulfill nature means to fulfill this true seed. To arrive at the meaning of life means to arrive at this true seed.

Knowing this true seed and cultivating it back to its original state, using this to cultivate essence, one can clarify essence. Using this to cultivate life, one can establish life. Therefore the classic *Triplex Unity* says, "It is easy to work with the same kind, hard to work with what is not of the same kind." This is like the need for fermented mash to make wine and rice to make gruel.

Bells Ring, Drums Resound

When a bell is struck it rings, when a drum is beaten it resounds. This is because they are solid outside and empty within. It is because they have nothing inside that they are able to ring and resound.

What I realize as I observe this is the Tao of true emptiness and ineffable existence.

True emptiness is like the inner openness of a bell or a drum; ineffable existence is like the sounding of a bell or a drum when struck. If people can keep this true emptiness as their essence, and utilize this ineffable existence as their function, ever serene yet ever responsive, ever responsive yet ever serene, tranquil and unstirring yet sensitive and effective, sensitive and effective yet tranquil and unstirring, empty yet not empty, not empty yet empty, aware and efficient, lively and active, refining everything in the great furnace of Creation, then when the dirt is gone the mirror is clear, when the clouds disperse the moon appears; revealing the indestructible body of reality, they transcend yin and yang and Creation, and merge with the eternity of space.

Marionettes and Kites

The reason a marionette can nod its head and a kite can fly into the sky is because someone is manipulating it with a string.

What I realize as I observe this is the Tao of the spiritual working of movement and stillness in the human body.

The human body is like a marionette or a kite, something inert; the spirit is like a person, energy is like the string. When the spirit operates the energy, the body is alive; it can be active, and it can be still. This is like a person using a string to manipulate a marionette or a kite.

The spirit operates the energy, the energy operates the body. Therefore it is possible to act and rest, it is possible to speak. If those who cultivate reality know how to control the energy by the spirit and nurture the spirit by the energy, then spirit and energy combine, and in the midst of ecstatic trance there is something, there is vitality.

That vitality is most real; gather and internalize it, and transmutation is endless. Moreover, it is then possible to manipulate heaven and earth, not just the ephemeral body.

Parrots and Monkeys

A parrot can be taught to speak, a monkey can be taught to act; they are able to do these things not because of their original natures, but because people gradually teach them.

What I realize as I observe this is the Tao of seeking teachers and finding companions.

Parrots are birds, monkeys are animals; when birds and

animals are guided by humans, they can speak human speech or dance human dances. How much the more so can humans, the most intelligent of creatures, ascend to the realm of lofty illumination if they have the guidance of enlightened teachers and the aid of good companions.

If you know enough to submit to enlightened teachers, associate with good companions, sincerely concentrate on clarification of truth, borrow their knowledge to break through your own ignorance, borrow their lofty vision to expand your own ignorant views, then even if you are ignorant you will become enlightened, and even if you are weak you will become strong. Then there is no reason why you cannot become a spiritual immortal and a buddha.

Ignorant students follow their own minds and act arbitrarily. Indulging in guesswork, they consider themselves bright and will not humble themselves. Thus they misapprehend the road ahead. Though they are said to deceive others, in reality they are deceiving themselves. This is looking on the great matter of essence and life as child's play. It is no wonder they strive all their lives with no attainment. Is this not a pity?

Elm Sheaths, Shepherd's Purse, and Wheat

In spring most things sprout, but the elm sheaths fall. In autumn most things become dormant, but the shepherd's purse and wheat grow. This is representation of negativity within positivity and positivity within negativity.

What I realize as I observe this is the Tao of combined use of benevolence and duty.

Benevolence is the soft path, based on compassion and love. Duty is the hard path, based on judgment and administration. If one is only benevolent, without duty, then love will lack distinction of right and wrong. If one is dutiful without benevolence, then judgment will become oppressive. Both of these states miss the center.

When benevolence and duty are used together, then there is decisiveness within benevolence, so that right and wrong do not get mixed up; there is flexibility within duty, so that there is no dogmatic rigidity. Thus the path of balance and harmony is not lost.

Desiring Water and Fire

When the weather is hot you want water; drink water, and you experience relief from the heat. When the weather is cold you want fire; if you have fire you will not be cold.

What I realize as I observe this is the Tao of mutual necessity of yin and yang.

The Tao does not arise from lone yin, does not grow from isolated yang. When yang culminates, yin succeeds it; when yin culminates, yang succeeds it: There is neither excess of yang nor bias towards yin; yin and yang are in harmony, firmness and flexibility balance each other.

Thus when one unified energy flows, the original source is complete, the mechanism of life is unceasing; essence can be fulfilled, life can be established. Unmoved by myriad things, not burdened by myriad affairs, one is beyond the world while in its very midst.

Otherwise, if yin and yang are isolated, separated from one another, firmness and flexibility do not match; the mechanism which gives life has already ceased, and no growth is seen. Instead there is decay, degeneration that culminates in death.

Heading South, Heading North

When you head south, you turn your back on the north; you see the south and not the north. When you head north, you turn your back on the south; you see the north and not the south.

What I realize as I observe this is the Tao of picking out the good and holding to it.

If people's minds are all good, what they see is good, what they think is good, what they say is good, what they associate with is good, and what they do is good. All of their actions, day and night, are good. They only know there is good, and do not know there is bad.

If people's minds are all bad, what they see is bad, what they think is bad, what they say is bad, what they associate with is bad, and what they do is bad. All of their actions, day and night, are bad. They only know there is bad, and do not know there is good.

If you see good you do not see bad, if you see bad you do not see good—falsehood and truth do not stand together, loyalty and treachery do not coexist.

Therefore developed people see good as something they have yet to attain, and they see what is not good as like plunging into boiling water. They preserve the Tao as though they were guarding a treasure, with single-minded will. Even though thwarted a hundred times, they do not turn back. They never change, even until death, and do not stop working until they have reached profound attainment of self-realization.

Cutting Weeds, Planting Trees

When you cut weeds, it is necessary to dig out the roots, for if the roots are not eliminated the weeds will regrow. When you plant trees, it is necessary to nurture the roots, for if the roots are not firm the trees will wither.

What I realize as I observe this is the Tao of eliminating the artificial and cultivating the real.

People's personal desires and habit energies are all artificial. The artificial is like weeds. People's basic essence and natural goodness are what is real. The real is like a tree.

When you get rid of the artificial, it is necessary to root out all personal desires and habit energies; only then will they not regrow. If you leave even the slightest pollution, eventually it will grow insidiously, gradually increasing and causing great harm.

When you cultivate the real, it is necessary to be constantly aware of the fundamental root of inherent natural reality, nurturing it at all times, irrigating it with the water of the spirit, keeping it warm with the fire of truth, not letting it be moved or disturbed, protecting it in every way, watching out for its safety in every condition.

When you nurture the root until it is stable and firm, when the energy is full and the spirit is complete, only then can you be immune to the influence of myriad things and the burden of myriad affairs. There will be no trouble after that.

Therefore when you eliminate artificiality, you must reach the point where there is no artificiality at all, just as when you cut weeds you must eliminate the roots entirely. When you cultivate reality, you must reach the point where there is no unreality at all, just as when you plant trees you must make the roots firm and deep.

An ancient scripture says, "As long as there is the slightest negative energy remaining, you will not become immortal. As long as there is the slightest positive energy remaining, you will not die." This is really true.

A Pitcher Full, a Pitcher Half Full

When water fills a pitcher, it overflows, and when it overflows there is lack. When water half fills a pitcher, then it does not leak out, and when there is no leakage there is always a sufficiency.

What I realize as I observe this is the Tao of filling and emptying, calamity and fortune.

When people are self-satisfied and complacent, presuming upon their ability and talent, knowing how to go forward but not how to withdraw, knowing how to be strong but not how to be weak, regarding only themselves and ignoring others, proud and arrogant, then eventually this will bring on calamity. Then their self-satisfaction will be useless.

When people are humble and self-effacing, deferring to others, conceding to others, not full of themselves, not proud in spite of their achievements, not arrogant in spite of their talent, always seeking out their own faults while honoring the excellence of others, knowing when they have enough, knowing when to stop, knowing both how to advance and how to withdraw, eventually this will bring on good fortune. Then they will rise from lowliness to exaltation.

Therefore it is said that the modest receive increase, while the self-satisfied bring on loss. Modesty is better than self-satisfaction.

Pottery and Decoration

Pottery has a basic constitution, and is formed without artifice. Decorate it with colors, inlay it with gold and jade, and though it may be beautifully adorned, it has lost its basic constitution.

What I realize as I observe this is the Tao of returning to simplicity and going back to purity.

The basic constitution of human beings when they are born is pure and flawless, but when it mixes with temporal conditioning, senses and objects are activated, intellectual knowledge opens up; added to this are accumulating habits and attachments. Those who like drink are deluded by drink, those who like sex are deluded by sex, those who like material goods are deluded by material goods, those who like energy are deluded by energy, those who like wealth and status are deluded by wealth and status, those who like sport are deluded by sport.

People pursue their ambitions with all sorts of scheming and cleverness, follow their desires with deceit and hypocrisy. All of their doings, all of their actions, are in pursuit of the false. They take what is painful for pleasure, take poison for medicine. Their original basic constitution is completely buried away. This goes to such an extreme that they lose their health and forfeit their lives without a care, bringing calamity and misfortune on themselves without even realizing it.

This is why the ancient sages taught people to understand the good and go back to the beginning, to return to simplicity and purity, simply to restore the original state.

When you restore the original state, you are clean and naked, bare and untrammeled. Without a trace of defilement, having shed clinging to objects entirely, this state is the embryo of sagehood, the seed of immortal enlightenment. This is what is called the real human being.

Having a Body, Having Energy

Whatever has a body assumes form and so must disintegrate. Whatever has energy is born and so must die. This body and energy are the basis of becoming and disintegration, birth and death.

What I realize as I observe this is the Tao of shedding birth and death.

People receive the energy of the temporal five forces, which form their bodies. In the body is stored the energy of the five forces. This energy in the human body acts up to become the five robbers, which are joy, anger, sadness, happiness, and craving. These five robbers are cohorts that strip away the real basis. Therefore what has birth must have death.

Perfected human beings transform the temporal and restore the primal. They rest their bodies in open space, store their spirits in silent tranquillity. Uninvolved with the energy of the five forces, they are unmoved by myriad things. They have no smoke, no fire, like dead wood or cold ashes; they have no form, no shape, like the sky or a valley. Heaven and earth cannot constrain them, Creation cannot rule them.

This is called taking over yin and yang, controlling the working of energy. You master your own life, and are not mastered by heaven. This is because heaven and earth can employ what has a body, but cannot employ the bodiless; heaven and earth can employ what has energy, but cannot employ what has no energy; heaven and earth can employ what has mind, but cannot employ the mindless.

If you are mindless, then you have no energy; if you have no energy, you have no body—there is only open space. What can heaven and earth do to open space? As far as causing birth and death, formation and disintegration, they can only cause birth and death, formation and disintegration of the body and energy—how can they cause birth and death, formation and disintegration of that open space?

An Empty Valley Transmitting a Voice

When a person shouts in an empty valley, there is a reverberation of sound. In folklore this is called the valley spirit. Because it has a voice but no form, it is called the spirit of the valley.

What I realize as I observe this is the Tao of nurturing the spirit in emptiness.

If people can be empty within, this is the valley. Within emptiness there is a point of spiritual energy, hidden inside; this is the spirit.

This valley is tranquil and unperturbed, this spirit is sensitive and effective. Only the valley can be spiritual—without the valley there is no spirituality. The marvel of the spirit is only in the valley.

People of the world are full of personal desires that block up the spiritual opening, polluting it in a hundred ways—how can they have a valley? Since they do not have the valley, they are confused and troubled, like drunkards or dreamers; their spiritual energy wanes away, so how can they have the spirit? Once they have lost the spirit, even though alive they are as if dead.

If you can sweep away all entanglements and wash away accumulated obsessions, so as to be clean and naked, bare and free, with nothing at all, then in that empty valley there will naturally be something indefinable with essential vitality, a nonpsychological spirit that is responsive, effective, and wise. Let go, it fills the universe; wrapped up, it is stored in secrecy. Thereby one can be a peer of heaven above and earth below.

Scale and Ruler

To weigh something you need to use a scale. Put something on a scale and you know how much it weighs. To measure something you need a ruler. Put something next to a ruler and you know how long it is.

What I realize as I observe this is the Tao of operating the firing process of the medicinal ingredients.

The medicinal ingredients are the two energies, yin and yang. The firing process is the practical course of cultivation. Correct balance, not being one-sided, is like a scale; order in advance and withdrawal is like a ruler.

When you cull yin and yang energies according to the rule of correct balance, they match each other in gravity, neither too much nor too little—then the medicinal substances are sufficient. When you operate the firing process of practical cultivation according to the law of order in advance and withdrawal, the length of time is measured, there is advance and there is withdrawal, the work is accomplished in one attempt—then the firing process is successful.

The weight of the medicinal ingredients is all a matter of correct balance. The order of the firing process is all a matter of advance and withdrawal. If you can be balanced and correct, if you know when to advance and when to withdraw, then the medicinal ingredients are both real, the firing process is accurate, and the great Tao is easy to attain.

To know when to hurry and when to relax, to distinguish what bodes well from what bodes ill, is a matter of expert judgment. To understand when to go forward and when to retreat is impossible for the ignorant. The medicinal ingredients and the firing process are not easy to know.

Raft and Net

To cross a river you need a raft; once the river has been crossed, the raft can be left behind. To catch fish you need a net; once the fish are caught, the net may be put away.

What I realize as I observe this is the Tao of using techniques to extend life.

Techniques are methods, methods of cultivating reality. Once yang has peaked in people, giving rise to yin, every day a hole is punctured in their completeness—the six senses rebel, the five forces damage each other, the three parasites make trouble within, the seven feelings run amok outside. This cuts away at the spiritual root day by day, until it is nearly gone.

Unless you have the great method of overcoming the dragon and conquering the tiger, the expert skill to turn the dipper handle, how can you destroy aberrant energy, how can you restore sane energy to wholeness? This is why the method is necessary.

The great Tao is natural and spontaneous, without artifice—why is it necessary to use a method of deliberate action? The reason it is indeed necessary to use the method is to get rid of degeneracy. When all degenerations are effectively done away with, then the method is not needed, just as a raft needed to cross a river is to be left behind once the river is crossed, and a net needed to catch fish is to be put away once the fish have been caught.

This is the meaning of using a method and not using a method. The same thing is true of using techniques to extend life—when life has been extended, then the techniques are no longer used. It is only before life has been extended that it is necessary to use techniques to take over Creation, reverse the working of energy, and shift the polar star. Only then can essence and life depend on oneself and not on heaven, so that one transcends the world and its forces.

Hibernating Insects Returning to Life

At the end of autumn, insects go into hibernation. In the spring, they return to life. Their rebirth is based on their hibernation.

What I realize as I observe this is the Tao of finding life in the midst of death.

The reason people do not attain lasting life is that they are unable to die first. To die means to make the human mentality die, to live means to make the mind of Tao live.

The heart is led around by emotions, desires, feelings, and perceptions. It is drawn by all sorts of perverse influences. Gangs of foxes and dogs invade and damage the mind of Tao. Thus the human mentality lives and the mind of Tao dies. When the mind of Tao dies, sane energy fades away; essence and life are shaken, so that people inevitably die.

If you want to give life to the mind of Tao, you must first cause the human mentality to die. When the human mentality dies, the whole gang of pillagers dies of itself like a snake without a head. When it has been destroyed to the point where there is nothing more to destroy, the mind of Tao gradually comes to life and sane energy gradually returns.

This is what is meant by the saying that when the darkness has lasted a long time the light is bright. Returning to life from death is like insects returning to life after hibernating.

The Oyster's Pearl, the Hen's Egg

When an oyster forms a pearl and a hen hatches an egg, in both cases it happens because spirit and energy are not scattered.

What I realize as I observe this is the Tao of incubating the spiritual embryo.

The spiritual embryo is the embryo of sages, the original basis of our lives. When the original basis is restored, the spiritual embryo forms. This is like when an oyster has a pearl or a hen has an egg, but they are not yet completed and have not been produced.

At this time there is no room for forced effort. One should just keep the attention focused single-mindedly, not letting the water evaporate, not letting the fire get cold. Guarding against danger, wary of peril, incubate the embryo so that it develops from tenderness to firmness, from faintness to clarity.

Naturally there will be a tiny pearl, which bursts forth from the furnace of Creation. Pervading the heavens, penetrating the earth, up and down and across, forwards and backwards, it cannot be obstructed by anything, being one with space.

This is like the oyster containing a pearl, its energy not scattering, like a hen sitting on an egg, its spirit not leaving. When the firing process reaches its time, the pearl will naturally be formed, the chick will naturally emerge.

The Phoenix and the Peacock

A phoenix appears but rarely, so it is considered an auspicious omen. Peacocks are always showing off their feathers, so they are taken captive.

What I realize as I observe this is the Tao of concealment and revelation, good and bad fortune.

Those who are bright and presume upon their talent, proud of their ability, contentious and competitive, giving their thought and attention to artificialities, are prone to bring on bad fortune.

Those who are inconspicuous and disregard brilliance and wit, who empty their hearts and humble themselves, who direct their effort to self-refinement, tend always to bring on good fortune.

Those who bring misfortune on themselves are those who use their brilliance outwardly. Those who bring on good fortune are those who use their brilliance inwardly.

Outward application means accepting the artificial and losing the real, wearing out the vitality and using up the spirit, walking into the road of death.

Inward application means getting rid of falsehood and maintaining truthfulness, building up the vitality and nurturing the spirit, returning to the doorway of life.

Good and bad fortune, life and death, are directly connected to the internal or external use of awareness. Therefore enlightened people cut off externals to govern the internal, while petty people strive for externals and thereby lose the internal.

This is like the difference between the concealment and display of the phoenix and the peacock, whereby one brings on good fortune and the other brings on calamity. Surely we must be careful about how we use our awareness.

Midday and the Full Moon

At midday, the sun begins to set; once the moon is full, it begins to wane. This cycle of yin and yang, filling and emptying, waxing and waning, is an established, unchanging pattern.

What I realize as I observe this is the Tao of the cultural and martial processes in cultivating reality.

Before the original basis has been restored, you use intensive effort to summon it, causing it to grow and develop. Then when the original basis has been restored to completeness, it is like the sun at midday, like the full moon—yang energy is complete.

At this point, you should receive the yang energy with yin, immediately employing the path of flexibility to incubate it, getting rid of hard hot energy and preventing danger. Concealing illumination, nurturing it in secret, with undistracted unified attention, seal it tightly and store it away.

Using one part of yin to store each part of yang, do not allow any leakage. This is like the way the sun begins to set after noon, the way the moon begins to wane after the full moon. When the yang fire and yin convergence are both attained, the cycle is completed and begins again, with yang energy being reborn.

This is called the strong, healthy, unadulterated vitality. The spiritual embryo is completely formed, and there is a separate heaven and earth that is not of the human world. This is the primal within the primal. Go on to do advanced work, building up this vitality bit by bit, at first faint, eventually becoming evident, and this becomes the unknowable sanctity that is called spirit.

The Dreaming of the Sleeper

When a sleeper dreams, he sees things that make him joyful, angry, sad, and happy—scenes of wealth, nobility, fame, and gain. The dreamer takes these to be real, and does not know he is dreaming them.

What I realize as I observe this is the Tao of depth of practical power in cultivation of reality.

People's minds are deluded by the energies of alcohol, sexuality, and possessions; their natures are clouded by emotions and desires. Inwardly and outwardly artificial, they completely lose their reality. If those who cultivate reality have any pollution at all that they are unable to dissolve away, even if the great Tao is in sight, they cannot completely attain it.

This is because the root of the trouble has not yet been thoroughly extracted. How can we test this? We can test it in dreams. If, when people are dreaming, the energies of alcohol, sexuality, and possessions cannot influence them, and emotions and desires cannot cling to them, if they are imperturbable and unshakable, pure and clear, perfectly lucid, not confused by anything artificial, only then are they seeing reality.

If they then go on to yet profounder work, so that they do not dream at all, then the root of trouble has been extracted completely. If they still dream at all, that means there are still accretions of sense that have not been done away with.

Therefore it is said that perfected people have no dreams. In those who have no dreams, the power of practice has reached its consummation. In those who have dreams, the power of practice is not yet consummate.

If you have dreams, yet while in the midst of the dreams you know they are dreams, this means the power of practice has advanced. If you have dreams and while dreaming are unaware that they are dreams, this means the power of practice is nil.

If you can actually reach the consummation of the power of practice, so that you have no dreams at all, then Creation is in your hands. Even though you sleep, it is like being awake. Even though dead, you are still alive. This is because what dies is the material body, while what lives is the spiritual body. What sleeps is the eyes and ears, what is wakeful is thc original spirit.

Commerce

Whoever would engage in commerce must first raise capital, and then must know how to use it. Only if one has capital and knows how to use it can one make a profit. If one has capital but does not know how to use it, or if one knows how to operate but lacks capital, one cannot do business.

What I realize as I observe this is the Tao of the twin function of method and wealth.

People who cultivate reality build up virtues and carry out undertakings, accumulate vitality and nurture spirit, remain consistently firm and stable, growing stronger the longer they persevere, never changing all their lives, working with a sincere heart. This is like accumulating wealth.

Seeking personal instruction from a guide to know the beginning and the end, understand when to proceed and when to withdraw, recognize when to hurry and when to relax, understand what bodes well and what bodes ill, and know when to stop at sufficiency. Proceeding in an orderly manner, finding the real medicinal ingredient, not deviating from the firing process, is having method.

Having wealth and having method, using wealth to provide for the Way, using method to practice the Way, through the twin use of method and wealth you see the effects of your effort step by step, until you finally attain great fulfillment. This is like a merchant having capital and understanding how to use it, reaping great profit in every enterprise.

If you have wealth but no method, or if you have method but no wealth, and falsely imagine that you will ascend right to the heights, then in trying to get ahead you will be thwarted and fall behind. Even if the great Tao is in sight, you will be unable to attain it yourself. This is like a merchant who has capital but does not understand how to use it, or who knows how to operate but lacks capital, ultimately failing to profit and prosper.

Therefore true aspirants to reality first seek in themselves and then seek from others, so that they will have both method and wealth complete. Only then will they avoid going wrong.

The Wild Monkey, the Stubborn Horse

The nature of the monkey is wild and uncertain, but if you leash it, it will follow human direction, unable to do whatever it wants. The nature of the horse is stubborn and intractable, but with a bridle and headstall on, it will follow human direction, unable to gallop off.

What I realize as I observe this is the Tao of rectifying the mind and making the intent sincere.

The stubborn mind of humans comes and goes irregularly, its home unknown, like the wildness of a monkey, without a moment's peace and quiet. The wandering intentions of humans arise and disappear inconsistently, suddenly here, suddenly there, like the stubbornness of a horse, never at rest for a moment.

The two of these are in cahoots, increasing human desires and obscuring their celestial reality. Because of this, essence and life are gradually destroyed, so the trouble they cause is most intense and the harm they cause is most great. So the first priority for practitioners is to rectify the mind and make the intent sincere.

When the mind is correct, then everything is open. When

the intent is sincere, then thoughts do not arise. When everything is open and thoughts do not arise, use this to cultivate essence, and essence can be clarified; use this to cultivate life, and life can be established.

But it is not easy to learn to rectify the mind and make the intent sincere. It is necessary to make a genuine effort in order to accomplish this. Genuine effort involves being careful of yourself, wary of what is unseen and unheard, consciously aware at all times, examining yourself again and again, not letting the stubborn mind or its arbitrary intentions stir at all, even in secret.

This is like chaining a wild monkey or bridling a stubborn horse, not letting them indulge in their natures.

Since ancient times the immortal real people have likened the mind to a monkey and the intent to a horse, because they truly saw that when the mind and intent are wild and foolish this is a tremendous obstacle on the Way, and they did not allow a moment's looseness.

If learners can actually control their stubborn mind and return it to rectitude, transform their errant intent and restore it to sincerity, then half of the Tao of essence and life can be comprehended.

Male and Female Reproducing

In the world, when a man and a woman mate they produce children, who eventually produce grandchildren, continuing from generation to generation. If there is a man without a woman, or a woman without a man, then solitary yin does not give birth, isolated yang does not promote growth—the productive mechanism stops.

What I realize as I observe this is the Tao of producing immortals and buddhas.

When people are first born, yin and yang are harmoniously combined and the spiritual embryo is perfectly complete. Then when they get involved in acquired temporal conditioning, yin and yang separate, and the spiritual embryo is damaged.

People of superior quality have a basic foundation that is deep and thick; if they meet adepts early on, before yin and yang separate, then they practice the Tao of nondoing and climb directly up onto the shore of the Tao, immediately equaling the sages in rank.

As for middling and lesser people, when their primal energy is full, the energy of acquired conditioning acts up; true yang and true yin are separated and do not interact. Thus the living potential fades away, nearly to extinction. If they do not first practice the Tao of doing in order to harmoniously combine yin and yang, how can they restore the spiritual embryo?

The method of harmonious combination of yin and yang is simply to cause yin and yang to return to one energy. However, true yang has wandered outside, and resides in the house of another; it has gotten lost and does not come back. It is necessary to make intense efforts to get it back. Do not be intimidated by the fact that the road is long—seek carefully, search slowly, and someday you will see its face. Then you can call it back to your own house and mate it with true yin.

Then when husband and wife are reunited, their intimacy is extraordinary. Naturally there is a point of living potential that comes from nothingness to congeal into an embryo. Incubate this for ten months, and you will have a body outside your body. Go on to do the work of suckling it for three years, and it will become a form when it clusters and an energy when it diffuses. Disappearing and appearing unfathomably, it becomes an adamantine indestructible body.

This Tao is no different from the way men and women reproduce human beings. It is just that ordinary fathers and mothers produce the material body, while the spiritual father and mother produce the real body. One is ordinary, one is holy—reproduction of humans and reproduction of immortals are as far apart as sky and earth.

The Real Human Sanfeng said, "Going along makes you mortal, going in reverse makes you immortal. It is all a matter of the reversal in between." Do you think reversal of the celestial mechanism is easy to know? The blind of the world who use the reversal of man and woman to practice the false art of gathering sexual energy can only form the seeds of hell thereby—how can they form the spiritual embryo?

Opening Doors and Shutters

When the doors are open, the air passes through. When the shutters are open, the light shines in. If the doors are closed, there is no circulation between the inside and outside. If the shutters are closed, the energy of the light is kept outside.

What I realize as I observe this is the Tao of great use of great potential.

People in the world today who practice Taoism go into the twisted byways of sidetracks, some closing their eyes and gazing into emptiness, some staying inactive in isolated and quiet places, some deliberately sitting and thinking of the spirit.

They think they have the Tao, but they have not realized that the Tao is the Tao of creative evolution of yin and yang of heaven and earth. This Tao, this Way, fans out everywhere in the universe, but this does not multiply it; it is concentrated in one energy, but this does not make it less.

All beings in the universe, animate and inanimate, the myriads of different beings, all live and develop on the basis of this. Everything and everyone has it. It is just that while people are in the midst of the Tao they are not conscious of the Tao, as while fish are in water they are not conscious of the water.

If you want to practice this Way, you must do it in the creative evolution of yin and yang of heaven and earth, realize its experience in the midst of all things and all events, and practice and hold it in the presence of all people.

This is work that is alive, effervescent, free, liberated, gloriously enlightened, true, and great. Do you think it can be attained by people who shut the door and sit quietly with blank minds?

If you want to attain the Way by shutting the door and sitting quietly with a blank mind, that is like shutting the doors and shutters and hoping to see the sun. What "way" does that accomplish? It must be the way of dark rooms, I guess.

Understanding Reality says, "Practice, mixing in with the ordinary people and integrating your illumination. When it is time to be round, be round; when it is time to be square, be square. As you appear and disappear, now reversing, now going along, no one can fathom you, since you make people unable to know what you are doing."

It also says, "You should know that the great recluses live in the cities and towns; why stay still and alone deep in the mountains?"

Only when you mix with the ordinary people, integrating illumination, living in the cities and towns, are you activating great use of great potential. This is the real function of practicing and holding the Great Way.

The Go-between

In conventional society when a man and a woman are married, they cannot meet but for the go-between. The go-between mediates between the families, and arranges the meeting. If people get married on their own, without the offices of a go-between, they are not considered proper partners in the eyes of society, and their relationship will not last permanently.

What I realize as I observe this is the Tao of harmoniously joining essence and sense.

Essence is inward, sense is outward. Let us say essence is yin, and is of the eastern house, and sense is yang, and is of the western house. When essence and sense are separated, yin and yang are blocked off from one another, like when the girl in the eastern house and the boy in the western house cannot meet face to face.

If you want to get sense to join essence, pairing yang with yin, without the offices of the go-betweens they cannot become one family.

The go-betweens are our true intent, our true will, also called true faith. Faithfulness can effect communication between other people and ourselves, faith can combine yin and yang. It is the first true treasure of those who cultivate the Way—from beginning to end, doing and not doing, culling medicine and working the fire, crystallizing the pill and freeing it from the matrix—the Way is not to be left for a moment.

Understanding Reality says, "If you have water and fire but not the two earths, even if you include the four forms you will not produce the pill. Only when both of you embrace the true earth will you get the gold pill to revert."

The two earths are the celestial earth and the mundane

earth, true faith in the middle of true will. The faith of celestial earth is the external go-between, the faith of mundane earth is the inner go-between, like the married couple that serves as go-between in the marriage of a girl and boy.

These two are the true go-between in our bodies. If you know this go-between and use it to harmonize essence and sense, then essence and sense will be harmonized. Harmonize yin and yang, and yin and yang then meet; the two join to make one family, and the gold pill very subtly takes on the impression of form.

Tasting What You Eat

When you eat something, you should chew it carefully and slowly. When you sense the sourness, sweetness, bitterness, and pungency, then you know the flavor. When you know the flavor, you eat what tastes good and reject what tastes bad. Some things you take, some you reject, according to your own judgment.

What I realize as I observe this is the Tao of thorough investigation of principle to find out what is true.

The science of essence and life is the most recondite, most profound, most subtle of learning. If your knowledge of it is not real, your practice of it is not right. Not only is there no gain, there is even loss.

Therefore it is imperative to study principle thoroughly first. When you have found out one part of the principle, you can do one part of the work; when you have found out ten parts of the principle, you can do ten parts of the work. Fulfilling your nature and arriving at your destiny is all a matter of determining the higher and the lower by thoroughly investigating principle.

The rule for investigation of principle is to go from the

shallow to the deep, from the rough to the fine. When you are done with one level, then you enter another level, finishing with one after another, entering one after another, until there is no more to set aside and no more to enter into, and you see what is underneath it all, recognizing the original source. Only then have you realized the ultimate accomplishment. This is like tasting food before eating it.

However, even if you have some spontaneous understanding, if it seems to be right but is really not, you will inevitably fumble, so it is still necessary to have the witness of someone of elevated awareness, to broaden your own perception, affirm what is correct, and reject what is wrong. Only then will you accomplish the task.

The *Book of Changes* says, "Investigate principle, fulfill essence, thus attain to life." Investigating principle means investigating this principle of fulfilling essence and attaining to life. If you do not know what essence is, or what life is, and yet wish to perfect essence and perfect life, what are you going to perfect?

Ignorant Taoists mistakenly consider essence to be in the heart and life in the genitals, or some say essence is in the top of the head and life is in the lower abdomen. Some concentrate on the genitals to cultivate life, some fix their minds to cultivate essence. Some keep their minds blank to cultivate essence, some practice culling to graft life. Some keep their attention on the forehead to nurture essence, some take pills and herbs to prolong life.

These people are all deluding themselves, and will eventually perish. People like this do not even know essence and life, yet vainly imagine perfecting essence and life. Is this not foolish?

Climbing a Mountain, Crossing a River

When you climb a mountain, you put forth effort with every step, not resting until you reach the summit. When you cross a river you take care with every step, not relaxing your attention until you reach the other shore. Even if you have climbed a mountain nearly to the summit, if you leave off that last step to rest your feet, you are still on the way, not yet there. Even if you have crossed a river nearly to the other shore, if you take a single careless step, there is still danger.

What I realize as I observe this is the Tao of physical effort to carry out the Way.

The Great Way is hard to know, so you are lucky if you come across it and know about it, and your efforts should be to really put it into practice, to actually tread the Way to its completion, thereby to repay your debt to whoever taught you about it.

No laziness can be admitted here, because the science of essence and life is the most important thing in the world, and it is also the most difficult thing in the world. It requires a stable mind and a firm will, "taking a stand without changing," "working by day and wary by night," getting stronger with perseverance. Only after that can you accomplish it.

Do not let a little bewilderment make you change your mind, do not let a little experience of its effect induce you to relax your work. Do not let a little material hardship divide your mind, do not be discouraged that your strength is insufficient. Do not have false imaginings about attainment of the Great Way, do not fear that the road is long. Keep going with steadfast determination, keeping your attention on the

Way, going straight forward, and naturally a day will come when you will arrive.

This is like putting out effort every step of the way when climbing a mountain, finally to reach the summit; like paying attention every step of the way when crossing a river, finally to reach the other shore.

Otherwise you vacillate and hesitate, not making any progress, perhaps diligent at first but winding up negligent. Even if the Great Way is in sight, you cannot attain it yourself.

Just think—ever since you were born, your whole inner and outer being has been a coil of mundanity. Though you have a bit of celestial energy, it is concealed and invisible. If you do not establish a sense of purpose so firm that life and death cannot change it, and use the great strength of an indestructible man of iron, how can you transform the mundane back into the celestial, climb a mountain ten miles high, and get out of the immeasurable ocean of suffering?

Moths and Worms

Moths fly into lamps, throwing themselves into fire and dying. Worms seeking warmth bring on their own death by exposure. Both of these creatures destroy their lives by their liking for light.

What I realize as I observe this is the Tao of heading for good fortune and avoiding misfortune.

Worldly people follow what they desire—they compete for fame, grab for profit, indulge in drink and lust. They take artificialities for reality, take irritants for pleasure. Day and night they struggle uncertainly, anxious and worried all the time, wearing out their vitality and spirit. They are not willing to stop until the day they die.

Such people are like moths flying into a lamp and burning

to death, like worms seeking heat losing their lives. This is what is called sending yourself to death without even being called by the Grim Reaper.

If you know in yourself the value of life, see through emotional entanglements and sensual cages, leap out of the net of fame and profit, be like a complete simpleton, learn to be a flexible, yielding ignoramus. Do not contend for what others contend for, do not love what others love. In all situations, lower yourself and honor others. In all affairs, do not be impulsive or forward.

Be like a fish submerged in the depths, like a turtle in the mud. Then criticism and praise do not reach you, calamity and fortune do not affect you. You live spontaneously without seeking life, you avoid death by not bringing on death.

This is a good method of heading for good fortune and avoiding misfortune. Nevertheless, foolish people consider external things more important than essence and life, bringing death on themselves.

The Silkworm's Thread, the Bee's Honey

Silkworms originally spin their thread for protection, not knowing that people will kill them for the thread. Bees originally produce honey for nourishment, not knowing people will take their lives for the honey. Both creatures want to enhance their lives, but in the process hasten their deaths.

What I realize as I observe this is the Tao of interdependence of benefit and harm.

People all fear death and therefore seek to live. Since they seek to live, they have to do something about food and clothing. They spend their days laboring mentally and physically in the ordinary world, accumulating money and supplies to enrich their lives.

Ordinary people would consider this enough to live on, but they do not yet realize that this is not enough to really live on. In fact, it actually hastens death.

How do we know it is so? The more serious people are about making a living, the less serious they are about preserving the body. They work day and night, resulting in unknown damage to their vitality and spirit, deterioration in their energy and circulation. They have already entered the road to death.

There is another type of person who does not know what brings death and what brings life. Faced with a hundred sicknesses, in the mornings such people are unsure of the evenings, yet they cannot give up food and clothing, wanting more and more the older they get, not waking up until they die, suffering confusion to the very end.

These people are like silkworms who bring on their own death by spinning thread, like bees who bring on their own death by producing honey.

People of great wisdom have a different way of preserving life. They do not keep their minds on food and clothing, they do not focus their attention on material gains. They give up worldly wealth to accumulate spiritual wealth, they slight the material body to nourish the real body. Nothing can move them, so what can profit or harm them?

Borrowing Seed from Another

What farmers consider most important is their seed. Those who have land and have seeds are all set, and do not need to seek to borrow from someone else. When it comes to poor families, however, they may have land but lack seed. In that case, they must seek from others to accomplish their work.

What I realize as I observe this is the Tao of borrowing seed in cultivating reality.

What is called seed here is the primal, real, unified energy. When this energy flows the usual way, it produces ordinary people; when it flows in reverse, it produces immortals. Therefore the alchemical classics and writings of the masters all regard this energy as the seed of reality of enlightenment.

This energy is inherent in all people, complete in everyone. But because it becomes mixed with acquired conditioning, negative energy develops and positive energy wanes, so that the true seed is buried, no longer visible at all.

Even though people with determination can clean the mind and stop all relations to objects, this is merely an empty field—how can it help hunger and thirst or rescue essence and life? This is why the seed of reality has to be borrowed.

Borrowing seed means one seeks from others. What belongs to others is not to be taken outright with empty hands, it must be sought courteously. With humility you gain the pleasure of others, and only then can you borrow the seed of reality.

When you obtain the seed of reality, you will see sprouts wherever you plant it, just as you see a shadow when you set up a pole. You will not waste any effort.

Cultivating reality without the seed of reality is like cooking an empty pot. It will never produce any real results.

Turtles Hiding, Fishes Lurking

When turtles hide in the mud, they come to no harm. When they emerge from the mud, people catch them. When fish lurk in the depths, they remain whole. When they come out of the depths, birds kill them.

What I realize as I observe this is the Tao of harming life and enhancing life.

The reason that people ordinarily cannot enhance life, and tend to hasten to their doom, is that they cannot hide their light and nurture it in darkness—confident of their intelligence, they use their talent and wit too much.

Intellectual brilliance, talent, and wit divide the mind and disturb one's nature, so that sane energy wanes day by day, and aberrant energy grows day by day. Eventually the root of life is shaken, so mortality is inevitable.

This is why adept humans do not give rise to thoughts from within and do not take in things from without. They appear to lack what they do in fact have; though fulfilled, they appear empty. They appear to be simpletons; they have understanding that they do not employ, they have illumination that they do not allow to shine.

Such people do not let the artificial damage the real, do not let externals disturb them inwardly. They only respond to an intuitive sense, only rise when pressed, only act when there is no choice. Though they are outwardly responsive, they remain inwardly unmoved. Though physically active, their minds remain unstirring.

When you meet such people, you cannot tell where they are going; when you follow such people, you cannot tell where they have been. Even Creation cannot constrain them, so what harm can befall them? They are like turtles gone into the mud where people cannot catch them, like fish lurking in the depths where birds cannot kill them.

When Oil and Coal Run Out

When its oil runs out, a lamp goes out. If you regularly add oil before it runs out, then the lamp can continue burning indefinitely. When its charcoal is used up, a fire dies out. If you keep adding charcoal before it is used up, the fire can continue burning indefinitely.

What I realize as I observe this is the Tao of grooming life to add to destiny.

Heaven and earth have the virtue of love for life. They only want people to live long, they do not want people to hasten death. What happens, however, is that people bring death on themselves and attribute that to fate. This is foolish.

Observe how myriad beings are born in spring, grow in summer, mature in autumn, then go dormant in winter, only to be born again in spring and grow again in summer. Those who live on undying are those who follow the natural order of the four seasons, and do not do anything extra. This is why they can live on.

Only humans have the same energy of yin and yang and the five forces but cannot follow it naturally. They cultivate unnecessary habits, take pain for pleasure, take poison for medicine. Greedily and gladly following their desires, they chop away at the root of life. Eventually their vitality and spirit wear out, their real consciousness fades away, just as a lamp goes out when the oil is gone, and a fire goes out when the charocal is used up. They will only come to the brink of extinction.

If people are really beyond the world, they consider essence and life important. They protect their vitality and spirit as one would protect gold and jade. They take care of the true consciousness as one would take care of rare gems. They do not set foot in a pit of fire, they do not show up in the arena of right and wrong.

At all times they set their minds on what is fundamental and focus their thoughts on the meaning of the Way. They are careful about what goes on inside them, and prudent about what they do in the outside world. They store their spirit and energy.

This is what is meant by the saying that enlightened people work on the fundamental; when the fundamental is established, the way comes into being. This is like adding oil to keep a lamp from going out, like adding charcoal to keep a fire burning. Those without life can have life, the unborn can live forever. Is the question of whether to live or die to be left up to heaven alone?

The Lotus in the Mud, the Chrysanthemum in the Frost

The stem of the lotus is hollow, so on emerging from the mud it is extraordinarily clean. The flower of the chrysanthemum is late, so on meeting the autumn frost it is extraordinarily fresh. When the inside is hollow, then outside things cannot leave their mark; when the flower is late, the energy is full and resistant to cold.

What I realize as I observe this is the Tao of cultivating the inward and being immune to externals.

The reason Creation can constrain us, the reason things can influence us, the reason calamity can harm us, is not that Creation can actually constrain us, or that things can actually influence us, or that calamity can actually harm us—it is all because we get emotional about what we experience. Encounters with things arouse our minds, like wind rousing waves in whatever direction it blows. If we know how to go ahead but not how to stay behind, if we know how to be forceful but not how to be yielding, we constrain ourselves, influence ourselves, and harm ourselves.

If you are actually able to be such that nothing occurs to you and not a single thought arises, always clear and calm, impervious to outside things, immune to external influences, you will be like a lotus that has emerged from the water, unstained by dirt. If you are actually able to hold back your talent and wit, being skillful but appearing clumsy, being wise but appearing ignorant, acting unobtrusively, first to yield flexibly, then calamity and fortune cannot reach you, criticism and praise cannot affect you. You will be like the chrysanthemum in autumn coming through the frost and cold.

The Lamp Cover and Brazier Screen

If a lamp has no cover a draft will put it out, but if the lamp is enclosed in a cover, it will not go out even if there is a gust of breeze. If a brazier has no screen it will get dusty, but if the brazier is screened it will not be fouled even by flying dust.

What I realize as I observe this is the Tao of safeguarding the foundation of consciousness.

Our conscious awareness is like a lamp or a brazier, awareness of reality is like a lamp glass or a brazier screen. If conscious awareness is not covered and protected by awareness of reality, the discriminating spirit will use consciousness to produce illusions, so it will be influenced by objects. Then the artificial will be in charge, the real will withdraw; aberrant energy will cover up sane energy. Like a lamp being extinguished, like a brazier being fouled, we lose our original selves.

If conscious awareness is mated with awareness of reality, and awareness of reality is used to control conscious awareness while conscious awareness is used to follow awareness of reality, then the discriminating spirit has no way to emerge, the energy of consciousness has no way to fly.

When the root basis is firm and stable, it may enter water

without drowning, enter fire without burning. No pernicious external influences can harm it. This is like when a lamp has a cover and so does not go out, like when a brazier has a screen and so is not fouled by flying dust.

Roundness and Squareness

Things that are round roll, things that are square remain still. The round cannot remain stationary, the square cannot roll around—each has its own nature.

What I realize as I observe this is the Tao of using roundness and using squareness.

Roundness means being in the center of the compass. In the center of the compass, you respond adaptively according to the situation—you can go up or down, be high or low, act or be still, not clinging to one rule or method.

Squareness means being in the center of the square. In the center of the square, right and wrong are not confused—you do not behave disrespectfully, do not act unjustly, do not live in a way you should not, being inwardly autonomous.

When you can be round and can be square, following the rules of the compass and square, then you do not fall into stagnant fixation or random suggestibility. Outwardly you are lively and active, inwardly you are calm and sure.

Using things of the world to cultivate the Tao, using human events to complete the Way to Heaven, you plant lotuses in a fire, haul a boat through muddy water, appearing and disappearing according to the time, active or passive as appropriate to the situation. Even the spirits of sky and earth cannot fathom you—how much less can your fellow human beings.

The people of the world who can be round but cannot be square, or who can be square but cannot be round, are like inert objects that are square or round, good for one thing but not for another. Right and wrong are mixed up in them—how can they attain the Great Tao?

Therefore practitioners of the Tao need to include both squareness and roundness, for only this is the true domain of great effective action.

A Broken Pot, a Leaking Jar

When a pot is broken, repair it and you can use it to cook as before. When a jar leaks, fix it and you can use it to hold water as before.

What I realize as I observe this is the Tao of recreating what has been ruined.

When people are first born, their three treasures—vitality, energy, and spirit—are a solid whole. Then when the cognitive consciousness opens up, these treasures leak out through the senses. They are infected by the germs of emotionalized action, playthings of parasites. Their sense experiences wear them down, their attraction to stimulation deludes their natures; greed, anger, folly, and attachment drain them of reality.

Chipped away by day and by night, the three treasures dwindle away; the whole body is sick, inwardly and outwardly spoiled. The original complete treasure has been made into a rotten, worthless object—just like a broken pot or a leaking jar, it is a useless vessel.

If you are like this but become aware enough to take a serious look at yourself and change your attitude, disregard everything except the restoration of your birthright, the most important thing there is for anyone, the matter of essential life; act on this in a genuinely real manner, one by one sweeping away everything acquired, withdrawing your aura, holding your thoughts fast, abandoning the false while keeping the real, eliminating the aberrant and supporting the true, increasing daily in accomplishment while diminishing daily for the Way.

Increase what is to be increased, diminish what is to be diminished, until you reach the point where there is nothing more to increase and nothing more to diminish. Then you will naturally not leak vitality, so your vitality will be whole; you will not waste energy, so your energy will be whole; you will not belabor your spirit, so your spirit will be whole. What you have lost, you will regain; what was ruined will be recreated.

Then you will be what you were before: something whole and complete, just as a broken pot that has been repaired is again a fine pot, and a leaking jar that has been repaired is again a fine jar.

Nevertheless, people who are broken and leaking themselves are not aware of their misery. They take the false to be real, chopping away at their very lives day and night, breaking themselves down until the day when the pillars rot and the walls crumble, and they have nowhere to rest.

The Mindlessness of the Infant

A fierce tiger will not harm an infant, a hungry hawk will not grab an infant. How can it be like this? Because the infant is mindless.

What I realize as I observe this is the Tao of the subtle function of mindlessness.

The reason people cannot attain the Way is always because they have minds. Having a mind means having an ego, which means seeing others as others and self as self.

When you view yourself as separate from others, you

seek advantage for yourself without regard for loss to others. You become crafty and wily, your personal desires multiply at random. Your natural goodness is lost.

If you cannot even accumulate virtues, how can you presume to imagine realization of the Way?

This is why true seekers of the Way make haste to overthrow egoism and abandon selfish behavior. In their lives and response to the world, they regard themselves and others impartially, and regard all classes as equal. Dealing with things as they arise, true seekers respond to them but do not take them in; they pass by and do not linger. They handle all sorts of situations without minding.

Not minding, they are egoless. Being egoless, they are inwardly pure. Being inwardly pure, they are flawlessly clear, wholly integrated with the design of nature.

This is called mystic virtue. Mystic virtue is formless and traceless, unseen and unheard—only thus do you share in the virtues of heaven and earth, the brilliance of sun and moon, the order of the four seasons, and the luck of the ghosts and spirits. Creation cannot constrain you, myriad things cannot harm you.

The infant is without conscious discernment or cognition—it is simply mindless, and nothing can harm it. How much more so is mindlessness that is both substantial and functional, in which both the Way and its power are complete—how could any external afflictions invade it?

Building a Foundation and Raising a House

The question of how long a house will last is all a matter of the first part to be built, the foundation. If the foundation and ground are firm and solid, the house will be stable and long-lasting. If the foundation and ground sink, the house will eventually tilt. This is an established principle.

What I realize as I observe this is the Tao of working on the basis of cultivating reality.

The first priority in cultivating reality is to refine the self and control the mind. When you refine yourself, selfish desires leave; when you control the mind, your will becomes firm.

When selfish desires leave and the will is firm, then the basis is secure and unshakable. Now if you combine the four forms, assemble the five forces, usurp yin and yang and take over Creation, cultivate essence and cultivate life, going straight ahead to arrive at profound self-realization, you will benefit wherever you go. This is like making the foundation firm, so that it will bear the weight of wood, stone, and tile.

If the basis is not firm, and the will is not single-minded, you will go willy-nilly from one thing to the next, diligent in the beginning but lazy in the end, losing what you do over and over again, falling behind in your eagerness to get ahead, wasting your strength. This is like the foundation listing, so that even if the house is still upright, it will eventually lean and tilt.

The Alchemical Workshop and Vessels

An alchemical workshop is needed for refining elixir, vessels are needed to hold the medicines. Without an alchemical workshop and vessels, there is no place to put the furnace and cauldron, no place to store the medicines. The alchemical workshop and vessels are essential to chemists.

What I realize as I observe this is the Tao of borrowing the artificial to cultivate the real.

The physical human body is like an alchemical workshop,

the organs in the body are like vessels. The physical body has a real body hidden in it, the organs have five forces hidden in them. Cultivating reality does not mean cultivating the physical body and its organs; it means cultivating the real body and refining the five forces. It is simply a matter of borrowing this artificial body and its organs to cultivate the forces of the real body.

What is reality? The real five forces are referred to as metal, wood, water, fire, and earth. The heart is associated with fire, whose virtue is courtesy. The kidneys and genitals are associated with water, whose virtue is intelligence. The lungs are associated with metal, whose virtue is justice. The liver is associated with wood, whose virtue is humaneness. The spleen is associated with earth, whose virtue is truthfulness.

Wood, metal, fire, water, and earth are the essences of the five forces; humaneness, justice, courtesy, intelligence, and truthfulness are the virtues of the five forces. These are primally inherent realities.

When the spirit hidden in the heart bursts out as delight, the vitality hidden in the genitals bursts out as sorrow, the mundane soul hidden in the lungs bursts out as anger, the heavenly soul hidden in the liver bursts out as joy, and the intent hidden in the spleen bursts out as desire, these are temporally acquired artificialities.

After people are born, the primal is mixed into the temporal, and the temporal is mixed into the primal. Considering this mixture and adulteration, if we do not refine away acquired artificialities, then the primal will not return. If we borrow the temporal to refine the primal while using the primal to transform the temporal, when the temporal is completely transformed and the primal is completely whole, this frees a radiant pearl whose light pervades heaven and penetrates earth.

Then you may soar straight up or go straight ahead, go against or go along—everywhere is the Way. When your achievements are complete and your practices are fulfilled, you break through space, fly to heaven in broad daylight, and shed the flesh-and-blood skin bag, which is now as useless as the alchemical workshop and vessels once the elixir has been perfected.

Ignorant people who do not know the metaphors used on the Way make wild assumptions and follow wilder practices. This is what is meant by the saying that if there is no seed of reality in the cauldron, it is like boiling an empty pot. Ancient immortals have said not to cling to this body as the Way; you should know there is a body beyond the body. Worldlings who work on their physical bodies, as well as those who worry about their ovens and minerals, are fools.

Caterpillars and Polliwogs

Caterpillars weave cocoons, polliwogs form from cells; eventually the cocoons break open to produce moths, the cells develop to produce frogs.

What I realize as I observe this is the Tao of liberative transformation of the spiritual embryo.

Those who cultivate reality assemble the five forces, join the hundred spirits, merge with the ultimate; one energy coalesces, whole and pure, not consciously cognized. Now the spiritual embryo has form, like when the caterpillar weaves its cocoon or the polliwog forms its cell.

Store the spirit and energy away in mystical darkness, and the bit of spiritual root will grow from faintness to clarity, from softness to strength. When the process is complete, suddenly you will break through space to reveal the pure spiritual body, leaping beyond the worlds. This is like when the caterpillar, having transformed into a moth, breaks out of its cocoon and flies away, or like when the polliwog becomes a frog and leaps. There is a body beyond the body, another world.

Therefore the aftermath of accomplishment of the Way is sometimes referred to as developing the power of flight, and sometimes called shedding the shell and becoming real. These expressions mean that you reproduce a real body inside your physical body. This real body is inherent in everyone, but people are fooled by the objects of their senses, deluded by illusory appearances, so they do not recognize the real body, even though it is right there.

Anyone who can recognize the real body and earnestly cultivate it can produce substance where there was none, produce form where there was none, undergo liberative transformation and become an immortal with an indestructible body.

The Racehorse and the Nag

A racehorse, a swift runner, can travel hundreds of miles in a day. A nag, ambling along, takes ten days to cover the same distance. Although one is fast and one is slow, yet what they achieve is the same.

What I realize as I observe this is the Tao of the relative speed of effective work.

Generally speaking, people are sharp or dull by nature, greater or lesser in strength. If people who are dull by nature want to emulate those who are sharp by nature, or those of little strength want to emulate those of great strength, they will be unable to keep up, and will injure themselves by the strain.

Therefore a complete sage said that those who are born

knowing are the best, those who know by learning are next, and those who learn the hard way are next after that. When it comes to the knowledge itself, however, that is one. Some may carry this out calmly, some may carry it out swiftly, some may carry it out forcibly. When it comes to the achievement, however, that is one. Among these three kinds of people, it may be difficult for some and easy for others, slow for some and fast for others, but all are able to know the Tao and attain the Tao.

The only trouble is when people have no will. Without will, not only is it impossible to act on the Tao, it is impossible even to know it. If you have the will, study it widely, question it closely, ponder it carefully, understand it clearly, carry it out earnestly; multiply the efforts of the ordinary person a hundredfold, and you can actually master this Tao. Even if you are ignorant you will become enlightened, even if you are weak you will become strong—no one who has done this has ever failed to reach the realm of profound attainment of self-realization.

Nevertheless, there are many Taoists in the world who cannot with a true heart regard essence and life as most important. They talk about the virtues of the Tao, but in their hearts they are criminals and gangsters. They want their imaginings of the Tao, and they want their greedy ambitions too. They are easily angered and unreceptive.

The intellectuals among them depend on their ability to memorize a few "spiritual" sayings, and think they have the Way. Consequently they disregard others and will not seek enlightened teachers or visit capable friends, thus mistaking the road ahead.

The dull ones do not know to investigate principles, and do not distinguish the false from the true. Having studied some "side-door" practices, playing around on twisted byways, they also think they have the Way, and will not go to high illuminates for verification, thus holding to their routines all their lives, trapped in unbreakable fixations.

People like these types do not really think about the matter of essence and life as the single most important thing in the world, and the cultivation and maintenance of essence and life to be the single most difficult thing in the world. How can this be easily known, or easily accomplished?

This is why those who study Taoism may be as numerous as hairs on a cow, but those who accomplish the Way are as rare as unicorn horns.

If you are a strong person who can be so utterly aloof of all things as to step straight into the Way, like steel forged a hundred times, with an unrelenting will to visit enlightened teachers respectfully and to investigate true principles thoroughly, then it does not matter whether you are sharp or dull by nature—eventually you will emerge on the Way, and will definitely not have wasted your years.

Red Flowers and Green Leaves

Red flowers may be beautiful, but they need the support of green leaves. If there are flowers but no leaves, the flowers will not be bright; if there are both flowers and leaves, the flowers are yet more colorful.

What I realize as I observe this is the Tao of the mutual necessity of the Way and virtue.

The Way is to complete oneself, virtue is to benefit others. Cultivation of the Way is internal work, cultivation of virtue is external work. Among those who have embraced the Way since ancient times, there has never been one who did not cultivate virtue.

The Way is like flowers, virtue is like leaves. As flowers

are supported by leaves, the Way is completed by virtue. As flowers and leaves are inseparable, the Way and virtue need each other.

Ancient sages first practiced the Way and then cultivated virtue. Ancient worthies first cultivated virtue and then practiced the Way. The sages were those of highest wisdom, the worthies were middling people. The sages attained comprehensive understanding and transcended directly to the shore of the Way; for them practice of the Way was easy, so they did that first and cultivated virtue afterwards to complete the Way with virtue. The worthies had to strive before they could enter nondoing; for them practice of the Way was hard, so they cultivated virtue first and practiced the Way afterwards to support the Way with virtue.

Students of the Way with higher wisdom are very rare, hardly one or two in ten thousand; middling and lesser people are countless. Among the middling and lesser people, those with shallow foundations, small perceptions, great afflictions, and deep attachments must first accumulate virtue. Great virtue can overcome ghosts and spirits, can move heaven and earth, can affect people and animals. Use this to learn the Way, and the Way is easy to learn; use this to achieve the Way, and the Way is easy to achieve.

This is because the Way is the substance of virtue, virtue is the function of the Way. The furthest reach of virtue is called mystic virtue. Mystic virtue is profound and unfathomable, near to the Way, so it is easy to learn the Way and carry out the Way based on this.

Students nowadays do not build up virtue or do good works; when they happen to hear a saying, they immediately rush into practice in hopes of immortality, without discerning whether what they have heard is correct or not. Needless to say they will not attain reality. Even supposing they attained reality, there has never ever been a single immortal who did not achieve anything.

The Great Way is not transmitted to people without social conscience, not handed on to people without goodness and virtue. The clear mirror of a true guide reflects everything—how could a true treasure be given to someone unworthy of it?

There is another kind of muddled fool who does not know how to walk on the real ground and work in earnest. Fools like this may run into true teachers but will not respectfully seek teaching from them; instead they spout a lot of nonsense, imagining that they can take people in. When the celestial mechanism is revealed, they try to usurp the teaching by devious means. Also they are incapable of perseverence—after a few days they are already asking for transmission, and then when they do not get it, they leave with angry words and recriminations.

People with mentalities like this, rushing this way and that, are uselessly wasting their lives, never to achieve anything. What they do not realize is that the Way is not apart from virtue, and virtue is not apart from the Way. How can you ignore virtue and speak only of the Way? How can you omit virtue and practice only the Way? Those who would practice the Way must first accumulate virtue.

PART TWO

Refrains of Lament

Pursuing Dead Matter

The Tao has become obscure to people—who can clearly recognize essence and life? People compete for status and reputation, and cannot get free of emotional entanglements. They are skilled only in artifice and opinion. All people like this are pursuing dead matter. It takes an extraordinarily brave person to realize this, turn away from it, and wake up.

Values

The Tao is no longer really valued. The mediocrities and the ignoramuses all have their many taboos, and they are suspicious when they hear people talk about the Tao. When they see people practice the Tao, they criticize and denounce them. They pay no attention to essence and life, they do not nurture the vital spirit. They only crave drink and passion, to fill their guts. Few people walk on the road to heaven—most of them compete to savor the taste of hell.

The Blind Leading the Blind

The Tao is no longer understood. There is an endless number of side doors and twisted byways, constituting a few basic groups. There are those who are fixated on voidness and those who are attached to forms, and those who do psychosomatic exercises. There are seventy-two schools of material alchemy, and three thousand six hundred aberrant practices. Since the blind lead the blind, they lose the right road; they block students and lead them into a pen.

The Open Gate

The gateway to the Tao is open—anyone can come in. If you know how to change directions, the goal is near at hand.

If you can act with a straightforward mind, this is a spiritual treasure. By knowing the One you extend the life of essence; when you perceive the Two, you congeal the spiritual embryo. Since ancient times, all the enlightened have dealt with people, but there is hardly any good material in the mundane world.

Decline in Taoism

There has been a decline in the conditions of Taoism. How many Taoists know the true self? Instead they take fish-eyes for pearls. Many of them regard plant products as fruits of immortality. All of them have abandoned the normal and taken a liking to the strange. All of them seek happiness, but instead they bring on disaster. All who meet enlightened guides but do not humble themselves have already locked the door by themselves.

Seek Guidance

Taoism is in a lamentable state. Why don't people who study it make a careful and thorough investigation? The great matter that concerns us most intimately is treated like child's play, the principles of the sages are taken for granted. People are selfish and inconsiderate, full of arrogant pride. They want to be at leisure and are afraid of suffering, yet they imagine ways to immortality; they seem to imagine that greed for leisure and fear of pain are prescriptions for immortality. If you don't know how to empty your mind to seek guidance, how can you understand the real yin and yang?

Degenerate Taoists

Taoism is degenerate. Most students do weird things. They haven't even understood essence and life, yet they put on high and mighty airs. By their greedy schemes for patronage, they run up their debts. How can they digest the food they buy with unearned money? How can those who act in such a way as to produce faults know about self-discipline? Take a look at those confused insects—they have all spoiled the teachings of the Tradition.

Artificial Exercises

The Tao is natural. All forced manipulations and concoctions are in vain. Some people guard their minds and settle their ideas and thoughts, some people hold their breath and keep it in the abdomen, some people perform psychosomatic energy-circulation exercises. When these people come to the end of their lives and find everything they did was useless, they will resent the gods, also uselessly.

Dragon Head, Snake Tail

The Tao is forever. If you lack perseverance, don't set off at random. People ask about the Mysterious Pass the minute they enter the gate; they want to get started before they have even learned how. In the beginning they are diligent, but eventually they slack off, their wills are not firm. Openly pious while secretly devious, many incur blame. They only want to impress people by revealing the celestial mechanism; the unseen spiritual immortals laugh at them.

The Normal Tao

There is nothing strange in the Tao. People with a liking for the strange have already missed the road. The colorful symbolism of Taoist texts is just that—symbolism. Common sayings and proverbs accord with the Tao of sages. The foundation of wizardry exists in daily and nightly activities. The mysterious, marvelous Inner Design is perfectly obvious, but the ignorant do not contemplate it carefully.

The Invisibility of Taoism

The Tao has been obscure for a long time. The spiritual immortals from the Han to the Tang dynasties (ca. 200 B.C.E.–900 C.E.) all withdrew into concealment. Because people accept the false and do not recognize the real, the enlightened have hidden their light and developed themselves in obscurity. Even though they had compassion, there was no way to exercise it; they had mastered the celestial mechanism, but whom could they tell? When they met someone who really cared about Life, then they would speak their minds.

The Teaching of the Way

The Way of the Tao must be taught. If you do not meet an enlightened teacher, everything goes awry. A succession of adepts handed on revelations of the mechanism, a succession of lamps pointed out the primal. There is nothing real in the entire physical body, neither in the brain nor the belly—none of the myriad phenomena you may experience are the Ark of Truth. If you understand what is before birth, shortly you will be growing gold lotuses in fire.

Awakening

Awakening is important for the Way. If you do not awaken, how can you set out? First you should find out the source of essence on your own, then seek a teacher to be certain about life. The primal and acquired are very dissimilar, the inner and outer five forces are on separate roads. When you thoroughly penetrate the secret of the celestial mechanism, you may transcend the ordinary and enter among the sages.

Flexibility

The Way is in flexibility. To act with flexibility is the best strategy. If you are conceited, how can you climb the right road? If you are impetuous, how can you get beyond the ordinary human condition? Later life is a manifestation of the life you led before; retreat, after all, stems from advance. If you seek to attain the Tao with a competitive attitude, you are like a blind man jumping over a deep ditch.

Resolution

To attain the Tao requires resolution, cutting decisively through whatever holds you back. If you cannot put aside sentiment, it will bind you hand and foot; if you do not get rid of greed and resentment, your intentions will be base. If you want to cultivate the Tao of immortals, first shed banality. If you want to rise to the realm of sages, what you have to do now is eliminate what ails you. People who study Taoism or Buddhism yet cannot wrap up the complications in their lives completely and effectively are ridiculous.

Vacuous Dilletantes

The Tao lacks affiliates anymore. So many practitioners are merely skipping rope—with one or two Zen phrases they pretend to be great hermits, having done a little meditating they call themselves advanced sages. Such people are insubstantial, shifty, and vacuous; they just talk to delude others, but it is themselves they delude. Who among them is willing to wake up and seek the true tradition?

Opening the Mysterious Female

The Tao is not a petty affair. The ignorant are just wandering in circles outside the gate. They do not know how to seek the root of creation. They wish to get the secret whereby they can perfect life, but it is only when one enters deeply into the recesses of inner design that one sees reality. When you open up the mysterious female, then for the first time light is allowed to pass through. There is one thing supporting the universe, complete—if you can recognize it, you can transcend things.

The Usefulness of the Tao

The Tao is useful—if you know it, Creation cannot move you. Younger people should work diligently, for when they get old and decrepit, medicine will hardly help. When you learn the Tao, you can transcend ordinary categories; when you practice the Tao, you can climb up onto the foundation of enlightenment. Students everywhere are lazy, letting the time slip away until they have spent their whole lives wandering.

In and Beyond the World

Goodness is important on the Tao. Once you turn to the Tao, why fear old age? The spiritual immortals have left methods of grafting life energy, which aspirants should practice with a true heart. Going back to the root produces life-prolonging tea; turning the attention inward is a restorative balm. If you do not cultivate yourself in this life, how will you know what road to return on in the coming life? Harmony is important on the Tao—what is the purpose of quietistic escapism? One of the ancient adepts used commerce to complete the great Way, another nurtured the spiritual tree while serving as an official. To be in the world yet beyond the world is the road transcending the ordinary; detached from society while in society, one enters the lair of immortals. So many realized people since ancient times have refined themselves in cities and towns.

Trivializations and Bastardizations

Unfortunately the Tao is not apparent to many people. How many understand that it is permeated with unity? This one lectures on ingesting elixirs, that one talks about flying. People pursue trivialities, acting out their whims, their practice ignorantly mired in cults. All such people have abandoned the real and play with the false—after all, who among them can reach the true goal?

Sincerity

Sincerity is important on the Tao. Why do students not bring forth their true feelings? When people go into debt to try to expiate their sins by religious contributions, charlatans go after their goods. An enlightened teacher is like a parent who gives you renewed life, the secret teaching is like the citadel of highest happiness—if you are deceitful and contemptuous of others, who will explain the celestial mechanism to you?

The Marvel of the Tao

The Tao is a treasure. If you understand it, it can extend your life span. This has nothing to do with material alchemy. It is utterly simple, utterly easy, there is no difficulty involved. It is completely spiritual, true goodness. The ridiculous thing is that foolish people seek mysterious marvels, when they do not know enough to preserve the mysterious marvel that is actually present.

Nonreification

The Tao is based on nonreification. It is formless, imageless, impossible to draw or diagram. Listen for it and you don't hear it, look at it and you don't see it. Try to get at it and you've already lost it; to discuss it is a hoax. It is so vast it contains the universe, yet as small as a tiny pearl. There are so many people in the world trying to cultivate realization who nevertheless look for the way in psychic phenomena.

False Students

The Tao is profound and mysterious—is there anyone to whom it can be spoken of? People lack inner sincerity, and are often proud and arrogant. They are not transformed, but claim to be immune to the world. Outwardly they pretend to be mature, while inwardly they are thieves. If you behave like this and still hope to cultivate immortality, you'll waste your life and suffer the consequences.

Access to the Tao

The Tao is most noble, beyond subjective feelings and ignorant judgments. It cannot be passed on through ordinary lines of transmission; it cannot even be handed on from father to son. It cannot be bought, even for ten thousand ounces of gold. If you are wholehearted, without duplicity, then you can benefit from the Tao. Apart from those who have gone beyond categories and ascended to the skies, who can easily talk about the secret?

Worthy Action

The Tao is centered and straight. To practice the Tao it is imperative to rely on worthy action. Only when you are imbued with worthy qualities and also act on them do you become real. Without virtue in action, it is impossible to become a sage. When your inner qualities are great, ghosts and spirits will render occult assistance; when your practice is deep, misleading influences cannot stand up to it. Quietistic inactivists are ridiculous, idly imagining they will realize essence and life by blanking their minds.

Finding the Tao

The Tao is as deep as can be—who is willing to pursue it closely? If you don't go into the tiger's lair, how can you catch its cub? If you don't wash out the stone and sand, how can you pick out the gold? Lower your head and bore into the hole of open nonreification; carefully seek the heart of heaven and earth with firm determination. Suddenly you will see the original thing; everywhere you meet the source, all is a forest of jewels.

Near yet Far

The Tao is nearby, yet people seek wonderful doctrines far away. Right before your eyes you are always seeing beautiful golden flowers, in everyday life you have the seed of realization—if you can recognize this you will shortly master yin and yang, if you can understand this you will immediately reverse life and death. This is something you cannot guess on your own—the instruction of an enlightened guide is necessary.

A Long Road

The Tao is a long road—you need to find out where it begins and ends, and what the route is. When you cull medicine, you must distinguish true and false. When you refine medicine, you must know hard and soft. When you operate the firing, distinguish when to hurry and when to relax. When you form the embryo, carefully add and subtract. The slightest error results in an enormous loss; how can a few words express it?

Learning the Way

The Tao must be learned. If you don't learn the way, how can you return to great awareness? First recognize the crescent moon in the southwest, the hexagram *return*; then investigate the overturned bowl in the northeast, the hexagram *stripping away*. At the gate of birth of the self you stabilize the root of life, at the door of death of the self you strip off the skin shell. How many people are there on the road of birth and death, and how many among them can take hold of Creation?

Balance in the Center

The Tao is completely balanced in the center, not leaning to one side at all. Who can go all the way through on this

Way? Black and white fitting together make the matrix of the pill, the unification of form and openness is the true work. In the mating of female and male is stored the will for life, the balancing of yin and yang arouses a peaceful breeze. If people can understand the meaning of central balance, they will be known as great heroes, whether they go vertically or horizontally, go against or go along.

No Way to Fake It

There is no deception in the Tao—even a little bit of falsehood already sets you far astray. It is essential to detach from the energies of wine, physical beauty, and material goods. Aggression, greed, and stupidity should all be eliminated. With a true heart and a true will, exert your strength to the utmost in practice. Pretend to be deaf and mute, let people criticize you if they will. When you have no conscious knowledge, all objects are empty. If you want to ascend to a high place, first you should descend.

The Impartiality of the Tao

The Tao is completely impartial—it is not a question of social status, or whether you are rich or poor. Everybody has the essence and is able to return to the root; everyone has the spirit and can go back to youth. The business of realization basically needs real people to do it—if people are not real, all their labors are in vain.

The Parting of the Roads

The Tao is deep, but if you want complete realization you need to investigate it thoroughly. The parting of the roads of immortals and ordinary people is just a hairsbreadth; the doorway of life and death is like a buttonhole. Even a little bit of carelessness and you lose natural reality; the slightest attachment to anything leads you into a ghost cave. If you do not understand what is beneficial and what is harmful in this context, your thousand prescriptions and hundred programs will all bring on inner turmoil and sickness.

Precipitous Routes

The Path is level, but students' leanings take them on precipitous routes. Sexual alchemy is contrary to the true eternal Tao, quietism is not the great method. If you try forcibly to cluster energy and blood together, you will produce ulcers and toxins. If you fixate your vital spirit rigidly, you will enter a pit of fire. The single road to heaven is right before us, but we do not discern it clearly until we meet an illumined guide.

The Priceless Pearl at Hand

The Tao is priceless, a pearl containing Creation. In storage, it is utterly dark, without a trace. Brought out, its light shines through day and night. Becoming wise depends entirely on this—you need nothing else to be enlightened. So many Taoists seek at random, all the while casting aside the treasure at hand.

The Tao and Its Methods

The Tao and its methods go together. With the Tao and its methods, the root of life is planted. Nonintentionally gazing on the ineffable is the basis of the elixir; intentionally gazing on the opening is culling the medicinal ingredients. When the furnace and cauldron are stable, there are no mishaps. When the firing process is carried out correctly, it forms the spiritual embryo. This subtle operation must be taught by a guide—it cannot be performed on the basis of arbitrary guesswork.

The Inner Design

The Tao is hard to put into practice. The first priority is to find out its inner design. Where is essence actually stored? What ground does the root of life ultimately rest on? The five forces are not in the internal organs, the three bases are all predicated on emptiness. Fools do not study the inner design, so they are confused from the very outset.

The Taste of the Tao

The taste of the Tao is fragrant, but how many Taoists are willing to savor it carefully? When the four forms combine, this extends your life; when the five forces aggregate, you enter the realm of immortals. The spiritual light of the crescent moon is the basis of the restorative elixir, the true energy of infinite space is the medicine of medicines.

Find It or Forget It

The Tao has no beginning—the circulation of one energy is its true key. It is no use for common imbeciles to crave their own ideas of it. It only teaches those who arrive at it to preserve it nondeliberately. When you find it, put it back into the jade furnace, and forge it into a star merged with the source. If you do not understand this celestial mechanism, stop spouting off in front of people.

A Ladder to the Heights

The Tao is a ladder to the heights—those who can ascend surely are outstanding. They are constantly gathering life-prolonging medicine, constantly whetting the demon-killing sword. When the acquired is thoroughly sublimated, the primal appears. When the shell of mundanity is shed, the spiritual embryo is stable. The only thing is that students fear to work really hard, so when the end comes they scream and holler in vain.

The Unfathomable Tao

The Tao is unfathomable, the complete, unique absolute, with no back, no front, no before or after. Now hidden, now apparent, it is at once open yet formed. What the eye cannot see cannot be spoken of—try to aim for it and you lose it. The spirit realizes it spontaneously. Fools all search in images—how can they come near the realm of sages?

Immortality

The Tao is sublime and mysterious, a Great Way to transcend the ordinary and enter into sagehood. When people hear talk about attaining immortality, all are attracted, but when they hear about the hardship of the work, all of them burn. All over the world there are people who want to get rich on this earth and also leap into the clouds and climb up into the nine heavens, but I have never heard of a sage coming from among them.

Right at Home

The Tao is simple and convenient. There is no need to seek afar, for it is right at home. Transform yourself, and there you have the soul-restoring pill. Change your outlook, and there is the real shore of the Way. The reason the spiritual treasure does not appear to seekers is that they themselves will not allow it to do so—what a pity that false people spend their lives madly in sidetracks.

No Bias

The Tao has no bias—when essence and life are both cultivated, that completes the great restoration. In the beginning there is doing, to perfect the jewel of life; in the end there is nondoing, to understand the sky of essence. Four yins and yangs are divided into real and false, two stages of work have before and after. Gazing at the opening and gazing at the subtle, only then is there complete perfection—when there is a beginning without an end, this is an aberration.

Reversal of Time

The Tao is fivefold—energy divides into water, fire, wood, metal, and earth. When one changes into five, this obscures the original reality. When five are one, you see the progenitor. To begin with, it is necessary to distinguish the primal from the temporal, then it is imperative to carefully discern the door of life and death. The subtle secret is between accord and reversal—if accord and reversal are not distinguished, discipline is in vain.

Stupidity and Madness

The Tao is clear, yet this clarity requires you to sweep away all your clutter. At all times watch out for your own stupidity, be careful of how your mind jumps around. When nothing occurs to involve your mind, you return to true awareness. When unified mindfulness is purely real, you comprehend the great restoration. The ridiculous ones are those who try to cultivate quietude—as long as body and mind are unstable, it is madness to go into the mountains.

Independence

The Tao is independent. Independence means you have to love yourself. If you yourself are present, things cannot drag you around. If you yourself are absent, your essence is obscured. Ultimately, if you yourself are always home, even the king of death will withdraw in surprise. If you do not know this mechanism, then all the practices you may do will just get in your way.

The Source of Difficulties

The Tao is not difficult. Difficulty is due to students' not really studying. Deep attainment ultimately should open up wisdom; if you are single-minded, eventually you will break through doubt. If you find the primal energy, you can soon crystallize the restored elixir. Knowing the end and knowing the beginning, you penetrate the whole course. The result follows in accord with the cause, so let there be no obstruction.

Witness, Practice, Experience, Transmission

The Tao must be witnessed. Having witnessed it, put it into practice and you will not be fatigued on the way. Though you may awaken to essence on your own, this is not to be relied on; the science of life, transmitted by teachers, must be ascertained through experience. Innate knowledge must be completed by learned knowledge; if you have real material, you still look for a master craftsman to make sure. It is a pity that people who consider themselves intelligent get involved in twisted byways because they act impulsively on random guesswork.

The Original Real Human

The Tao connects with the spiritual. Once understood, it applies to everything, going beyond the dust of the ordinary world. Recognize the original formless thing, and forge it into an adamantine, indestructible body. This is most sacred, most spiritual—the three poisons of greed, aggression, and stupidity die out, there are no calamities, no difficulties, all seasons are spring. This method has no difficulty, it is really simple and easy; nevertheless, in this world there are few real people.

The Stateless State

The Tao has no state—its real description would be a stateless state. Tranquil and unstirring, yet sensitive and effective—call on it and it responds, in quietude it is clear. Gather it up and put it in the furnace of cosmic space, forge it into a staff coterminous with heaven. The true secret has to be transmitted outside of doctrine; those who have accomplished nothing and practiced little cannot even think of aspiring to it.

Don't Rush Blindly

The Tao is extremely recondite. The slightest deviation adds a useless burden. It is necessary that the ingredients of the spiritual alchemy be in proper proportion, and that the firing process be complete from start to finish. Only when you know what bodes well and what bodes ill can you safeguard the real. Only when you adjust it appropriately is your work successful. When you understand one part, you can apply that part. If you rush blindly into practice, your effort is wasted.

Don't Guess

The Tao is truly different. When you know it, it helps you wherever you go. Reversing yin and yang at the main door of the mysterious pass, revolving heaven and earth at the root of spiritual energy, picking up the luminous pearl under the red dragon's jaw, finding the vessel of truth in the tiger's den—these matters should be figured out in the company of spiritual immortals; they do not admit of the guesswork of the ordinary ignoramus.

The Real Body

The Tao is most real. First you should recognize the original human in detail. Seek the original essence inside the temperamental nature, look for the real body inside the material body. The difference between right and wrong is minute; it is only in before and after that remote and near are distinguished. The deluded all play in the physical body—they take the secondary for the primary.

How to Act

The Tao is extremely fine. Behavior has something to do with it. Control the mind, refine the will, guard against danger keenly. Work by day, be aware at night, always as if in peril. The moment you let yourself relax, your real essence suffers; any aim for leisure, and the door of life shuts. Practicing the Tao is like walking on layered ice—one wrong step and your whole body gets injured.

Mastery of Openness

The Tao is fundamentally open, but in this openness is a master. This is the true source progenitor that operates Creation, the great spiritual power that sustains essence and life. Entering into sagehood, transcending the ordinary, depends on its power; moving the stars, directing the North Star, it does not expend effort. It is imperative that you see what the master is really like—if you have not seen it, how can you be restored to youth?

Energy, Vitality, Spirit

The Tao is in the body. Within the body is hidden another person, who always accompanies you, whatever you do. Awake or asleep, it is always there; looking, listening, talking, walking, it is very very close. This is not the awareness of conditioned knowledge, it is the original sane energy, vitality, and spirit. If you seek this in terms of form or shape, you are mistaking the servant for the master.

The Subtlety of the Tao

The Tao is subtle. Ordinary people laugh when they hear about it. One turns the mechanism of evolution of yin and yang, bores through the primal opening of chaos, picks out the staff of nonattachment, and with it scatters demons. Whether to oppose or conform is up to the mind; on the peaks of a thousand mountains, one sings and hums forever.

Diligence

Diligence is important on the Tao. Seek the fundamental master, even if you have to forget about food and sleep to do it. Every thought sincere, you should be wary. Reflecting inwardly time and again, you should be careful. With deep attainment, you naturally climb the shore of the Way. With ultimate sincerity, you are certain to taste the fragrant energy. If you are insubstantial and lacking in will, how can you ever transcend the ordinary crowd?

The Uniqueness of the Tao

The Tao is unique, without duality—why do deluded people divide it into high and low? The great ultimate is originally a name for complete awareness, ultimate sincerity is itself the form of the gold pill. When you recognize that the principles of the sages are the same, you will realize that Taoism and Buddhism are alike. If you do not understand this and seek elsewhere, you will get involved in sidetracks, wasting your life in vain imagining.

The Multifaceted Tao

The Tao is multifaceted. I have experienced all kinds of Taoism, false and true. First I met a teacher who opened a clear road, later I met another who showed the great restoration. After more than twenty years, I finally knew myself; after a hundred thousand refinements, for the first time I climbed up into the Ark. If one does not persist in intensive single-minded efforts, how can one presume to muddle one's way across great rivers?

The Beginning of the Tao

The Tao has a beginning. To complete the beginning with the end is the message of the sages. Cultivate essence by way of life, and you then reach stability. From being return to nonbeing, and only then you rest. Give up halfway along, and you have wasted your effort; those who abandon themselves midway are not true practitioners. In many cases, the student does not recognize the real. If you recognize the real, what is the difficulty in comprehending life and death?

Prohibitions

There are prohibitions on the Tao. The stairway of essence and life is worth ten thousand pieces of gold. If you wrongly pass it on to someone unsuitable, a star of ill omen appears; if you lightly reveal the celestial mechanism, calamity hovers near. Students may be very eager to find out the Way, but their will is deepest after a true teacher has instructed them. People without the capacity for the teaching can hardly be brought along—when you actually meet a connoisseur, then you speak your mind.